Strangers Within Our Gates

Strangers Within Our Gates

East Meets West: Language, Religion, and Politics

Rev. Paul Boecler

To order additional copies of this book, contact:
Xlibris Corporation
1-888-795-4274
www.Xlibris.com
Orders@Xlibris.com
67075

Contents

Dedication

To my three Asian friends. They taught me more than I taught them.

Qian Xie

Chao-Nan "Miles" Qian

Nariyoshi Shinomiya

Acknowledgments

Thanks to the following:

Kathy Reister, who organized English as a Second Language course at Immanuel Lutheran, and nearly ruined it when she asked me to volunteer as an instructor.

Mandana Nakhai, my former colleague at Concordia College at Bronxville, New York, who pushed me into writing this work.

Gertraud Boecler, who supplied me with unfailing encouragement, some valuable insights, and a few vocables as well.

I should have preferred to place the full responsibility on these three women for all the flaws in this book. But that would be like blaming Florence Nightingale for the battle wounds on an army soldier. The truth is, all flaws herein are my own creation and sole possession.

Facing Off

The Van Andel Research Institute stands on the edge of a hill in Grand Rapids, Michigan, one in a complex of other medical facilities. Van Andel's modern five-story building draws your eyes to it like a magnet. You can see how proud it is of its good looks with its clean and straight lines, its contemporary, sleek, and gleaming appointments. A sheet of glass windows on its western side looks down the hill and out across a small parking lot on to the brilliant stained-glass windows of Immanuel Lutheran Church. Its Romanesque architecture and massive gray stonework betrays its age.

Begun in the 1850s by German immigrants, Immanuel, as I write, is celebrating its 150th anniversary. Van Andel, by way of contrast, opened in June 2000, the very month and year when I retired and moved to Grand Rapids with my wife, Gertraud. The two structures confront each other in age and appearance, like David and Goliath. They feel out of place side by side. They are not what you would call two peas in a pod.

The Asian scientists at Van Andel appear more like David than Goliath. There is a colony of them, almost all Chinese, one or two Japanese. They are bright and energetic young men and women, with special visas in hand, sporting their MDs and PhDs. I envy their slim and youthful physiques. They came with their native cultures intact. You could stamp Made in China across their politics, their economics, and especially their religion.

They are mainly Buddhists, some of them nominally so, much like their Easter and Christmas Christian counterparts. As scientists, they are wedded to the scientific method and skeptical of claims derived from divine revelation. "If they discover the cure for cancer anywhere," I was told when we arrived, "it will be here at Van Andel." It was an overheated and exuberant claim. But the researchers at Van Andel are devoted to the cause.

There are no Asians at Immanuel. The members are 99 percent English-speaking whites, sprinkled here and there with a few dark faces. It belongs to the more conservative of the two major Lutheran denominations. There are no female preachers, no women's names listed as members of the executive board. Its leaders teach a six-day creation and speak disparagingly of scientific evolution. Only a small percentage has ever traveled abroad. Few speak a foreign language.

Their Asian neighbors ignore the church bells, which call to worship. They are not apt to step foot within the impressive sanctuary for even a look-see. And the message of these Lutherans—supernatural in content, centering on the work of a young Nazarene, Jesus of Galilee, where once they say "God walked with men in Galilee"—well, their next-door scientists are skeptical of that, if not resistant.

I am a member of that church. And I believe its message. Could I ever find common ground with any of Van Andel's Asian scientists? For we live in two different worlds and from two conflicting cultures.

Getting Acquainted

In March 2003, Kathy Reister, director of outreach at Immanuel, mailed an overture to the chief administrator at Van Andel. It contained Immanuel's offer to teach English as a Second Language course. Kathy approached me to volunteer as a teacher. I concluded I was eminently qualified because there were no qualifications, only as she said, "Just a fundamental knowledge of the English language." I thought I could rise to that standard. "Not to worry," explained Kathy, "each student will receive a book containing words to practice for pronunciation, words to define, and short stories by O. Henry, Hemingway, and Pearl Buck among others. And the book has follow-up questions and exercises for the students to complete." Plus, she added that each instructor will have a teacher's manual, which includes innovative ideas for teaching and—thank goodness—all the correct answers to the exercises and questions. "It would be a piece of cake," she reassured. Sounded simple enough. So I signed up.

In the overture, Kathy indicated that the teachers would "share the Gospel" with the students. That worried me. I was a Christian, an ordained Lutheran minister in fact, and as such I was eager to share Jesus with people. But was ESL a subterfuge, a subtle device by Immanuel to score some points, jewels in the crown of the church's statistics under the heading "converts gained by the church"? I wanted none of that. If the occasion presents itself naturally enough, I would explain Christianity certainly, but there would be no attempts to convert, to argue, no arm-twisting. Not even an overt invitation to accept our faith.

Besides, what were we thinking? Did we suppose that these foreigners would not suspect this course for an underhanded trick to convert them? How would I react if, as a student in China, I would be invited to attend a Chinese as a second-language course taught by a Buddhist priest in a Buddhist temple?

Armed with that resolve, I arrived early for the first Thursday-evening session in the church's parlors. "Parlors" was a fancy name for the furnished basement, with classrooms and a large meeting room attached to the church's kitchen. I was dismayed to see on one of the three tables, arranged in a semicircle for the class, a pile of pamphlets, invitations to attend our upcoming worship services. Jennifer McGraw, another volunteer, was busy in the kitchen preparing some refreshments. I was relieved to learn, after a two-minute chat, that our attitude was the same. "What a mistake," we agreed, to begin with that approach. The invitations remained on the table, undistributed to our guests.

Eight scientists attended the first session. Kathy introduced me. "This is Pastor Paul Boecler, an emeritus at Immanuel." "What's emeritus?" they asked. They weren't proficient in English, much less Latin. Kathy and I had the past two years engaged in good-natured teasing. I kidded her about being grossly overpaid while putting in short hours and taking long naps on the job—a transparent untruth. She got in her jibe this time. "'Emeritus' means that Pastor Boecler is an ancient old-timer on our staff. You'll have to excuse his feeble absentmindedness." I feared they'd think she was serious.

Having preregistered, we knew their names and had their shortened versions printed on place cards, behind which they took their seats. I made a garbled attempt to pronounce their names. After repeated attempts at "Qian," my tongue produced "Chen." Later she told me, "Just call me Jane." But I stuck to Chen.

Chen was my Swan, elegant and graciously well mannered, tall—"I'm taller than most Chinese," she once told Gertraud—and slender like all the rest. They obviously had not grown up on McDonald's Big Macs and french fries. Married, her husband and three-year-old son remained at home, in Shanghai, which explained the occasional faraway look on her eyes, yearning for family and home. A classy dresser with long black hair, she bore herself aristocratically, which reflected her upper-class standing in China. Following in the steps of her mother's profession, she earned her MD and PhD and was clearly devoted to her father, a civil engineer now retired.

"But a swan can bite," as my daughter told me, based on her own experience. A postdoctoral PhD, Chen won a $50,000 grant for Van Andel. "But I get to keep only a $1,000 for myself," she complained. She was fiercely patriotic and defensive of her homeland. A neighbor had complained, she told me, that the Chinese had swiped our technology. "Well, isn't that so?" I said. "You Americans," she snapped at me, "you always think we steal everything from you." Chen was no pushover, no wallflower. She showed her teeth in defense of China if the occasion demanded it. Still, she was never obnoxious in support of her country. She was too gracious and cultured for that.

This Swan, though newly arrived in the States, glided around self-confidently, unintimidated by American customs, though largely uninformed about them. Yet she was eager to learn. Her generous laughter made my awful jokes sound funnier than they were.

Chen sat to my right, and off to the far left sat Shino, one of the two Japanese. Somewhere in the middle was Miles. A mischievous broad smile accentuated the dimples on his round full face. His jet-black hair, straight up and erect, filled his scalp. Like a brush, each strand popped up after he swept his hand across it. "Miles?" I asked. "How did you get that name?" A professor in China had asked him what he hoped to be someday. A millionaire. That hope in Chinese somehow got translated into Miles. I still cannot remember his real name. I never bothered to learn it. Everyone knew him simply as Miles.

Miles was a vast reservoir of information. "Chen," he announced to the group, "you know, she has lot of money." Chen wondered, much to her annoyance, how he had acquired that piece of personal information. "Would our visas allow us to visit Hawaii?" someone asked. "I don't see why not. It's one of the states. Well, let me think," I wondered out loud, "when was it that Hawaii entered the Union? I can't quite remember." Miles knew. "In 1959," he answered authoritatively, like the encyclopedia he was. After scores of reported miscellaneous pieces of information, such as this one, I concluded he had a near-photographic memory.

Chen asked, "Those writings in *New York Times*—do they ever criticize government?" (They often dropped the definite article and some indefinite ones too.) She meant the editorials and the articles on the Op-Ed page. "Of course, they do. They're not only about politics though," I explained. "They're about all sorts of issues. But, yes, they surely can be critical. In fact, some of them are." "Do writers give their names?" she asked. "Why, of course. Why not?" I answered. (Chen was currently in the dark about freedom of the press in the USA.) "We have articles like that in China too," Miles interrupted. "Do the writers add their names?" I asked. "They do, but they're not their real names," said Miles. "But *I* know who they are." It became clear why I invented a last name for him: Miles Who-Knows-Everything.

There was another side to Miles, however. Like an abridged, small-scale version of Mother Teresa, he was an unusually caring and compassionate person, sensitive to human needs. If Chen was the class's Swan, Miles was the Bumblebee, buzzing around in circles to help in various ways and places. He was the quickest on the draw to clean the dishes after our pizza parties, to arrange the chairs and table for class—and replace them afterward—to offer rides for visits here and there. He funneled his knows-everything into helpful medical guidance. After the Schiavo controversy, I brought my advance directive to class. He gave me his advice. "No, don't simply write, 'I do not want breathing machine support.' Add, 'For more than two weeks, if then.' Don't write, 'No resuscitation if heart has stopped working.' Add, 'If diagnosed as brain-dead for one week.'" With boundless energy, this Bumblebee was everywhere, suggesting, informing, and always, always ready to lend a helping hand.

I made my torturous attempts to pronounce the other names until I came, at the end of the line, to the abbreviated name of a Japanese.

Shino was professor at the National Defense Medical College in Japan. He was a rank above Miles and Chen as a scientist. He came, in fact, as a distinguished visiting professor for his two years at Van Andel. As Chen was taller than most Chinese, Shino was shorter than most Japanese—and skinny, not merely slim or slender. But what he lacked in height and weight, he made up for professionally being a Shaq O'Neil. His résumé glittered with credentials—degrees earned, honors received, scientific articles published, membership on government commissions, and so on—although his deliberate modesty and self-effacement kept that secret from most eyes.

Early each morning at the appointed hour, a telephone call arrived from Japan. On the other end were his two young sons and wife. His parents owned a liquor store managed by his brother, which accounted for what we both had in common: *scotch*! "I suppose your parents help your wife with your two children," I suggested because his wife with her own PhD in chemistry taught at a Japanese college. "No, they live too far away to help." "Doesn't your wife resent your absence, what with all the cooking, cleaning, the kids, and all that?" "Well, uh, yes," he hesitated, "but she complains about everything." Sounded familiar, a normal relationship, I concluded, much like an American one, similar to mine. Shino plainly missed his wife and sons and balanced his earlier put-down with, "She smarter and got better education than I ever did."

Shino was my Pool. There was depth to this Pool, filled with wisdom and mature insight. Restrained, calm, and in control, nothing rippled his surface. He was a clear contrast to my Bumblebee but a perfect fit for my Swan. Contrary to what I expected, Shino, not Miles her fellow Chinese, became Chen's close friend. We named Miles Who-Knows-Everything, but the claim was as suited for Shino. He had traveled widely throughout Europe as a young man—to Rome and the Vatican City, to Germany and the Berlin wall, to England and Westminster Abbey. He filled in more accurately the missing parts of Miles's advice and facts. Everyone listened when he talked.

Of course, he loved the Land of the Rising Sun. Nevertheless, he was not narrowly patriotic about his homeland, quite different from Chen. My opening nervous and knee-jerk remark about Japan's sneak attack at Pearl Harbor and America's retaliatory atomic bombs—which provoked a loud guffaw from Miles—embarrassed me. I quickly tried to save face by decrying war's stupidity and horrors. I even invented a partial defense for why Japan initiated hostilities. Shino was too well balanced to agree and was unruffled by my regrettable reference to Pearl Harbor. Happily, my Pearl Harbor comment created no angry waves on my Pool.

The original eight in our introductory session melted down in time to these three: Chen, Miles, Shino. The others left my class for various reasons. For instance, there was Dong Kong, sitting near Miles. "Do you know any Chinese literature?" he asked Jennifer and me. "A little, maybe," we said, stretching even that half-truth somewhat. "Have you ever heard of Confucius?" "Yes, sure, of course, we did," we answered more truthfully. (I was beginning to see how little *they* knew about us.) "Well," he continued proudly, "I am the umpteenth-generation descendant of Confucius." "Wow! That's impressive!" we said. Actually, we were faking that since we were not exactly devoted admirers of Confucius. Dong fell in love with a Spanish scientist here for a visit. He later followed his heart to New York City, transferring to the clinic where she researched.

Next sat Jacob Zhuang, who casually and matter-of-factly reported, "I am Lutheran." "A Lutheran?" I said, amazed. I knew that there were some Christians in China, a tiny minority in a 1.3-billion population—but Lutherans in China? This took me by surprise. "Yes, a Lutheran," he said, born and bred in China. (I was beginning to see how little *I* knew about them.)

There was another Chinese whose name escapes me and then Lu Sung. She was a brilliant scientist, they told me, who fluently spoke Chinese and Japanese though hardly any English. Her youthful face looked as if she was twenty-five years old, not the thirty-five that, in fact, she was, with a teenage daughter.

The next PhD was a Japanese sitting next to Shino. My ESL book was number 7, where the English was at the level of an early high school proficiency. This proved too challenging for these others in the original eight. They moved to a lower level with other volunteers, Jennifer and Mike McCarty, who was a Roman Catholic. I learned to my relief that Mike was also adamantly opposed to proselytizing. Mike and I became friends, sharing regularly our experience. I regaled him about the remaining threesome in my class: my Swan, my Bumblebee, my Pool.

These were my students. They were more than students, however; they became my friends even though we had as much in common as those two buildings that faced each other—the one where they worked, the other where I worshiped. They were an odd mixture, really, quite different from one another, even the two Chinese. They contrasted each other not only in personality, obviously, but also in religion and even in political outlook. If you were to ask me which one of them was my favorite, that would be as if asking which do I prefer most: oxygen, food, or water. If you removed even only one from the class over the next two years, well, that would be as if amputating my right arm. They kept my old engine humming in my retirement years, even as they are only living now in my memory. After each Thursday-evening session, I came home with some tale about them to tell Gertraud.

My Thwarted Lesson Plan

Not that teaching ESL was a cinch for me. They joined the class to expand their vocabulary, and I was not naturally gifted as a linguist. I stumbled over the meaning of some words like a blind man searching for lost keys. I worsened my efforts by defining a word with another word, which they also didn't understand and that evoked, "But what does *that* word mean?"

If I kept to the book's exercise in each lesson under the heading Definitions, I was on safer grounds. That exercise contained a list of words in alphabetical order. They were to match this list with a parallel list of simple definitions. "Use a dictionary if you must," I told them. They did. They came equipped with their Chinese and Japanese dictionaries, which rescued them when they were stuck at making a matchup. "Or use the process of elimination with the last few that stump you. You don't need to get them all correct."

Now, I had always planned a carefully structured and timed lesson. I was obsessively conscientious about following it. The initial ten minutes, for chitchat. "How have you been? What was your day like? Are the Americans treating you OK?" Then the first five minutes to practice the words under the title Pronunciation. "Let's say the words together . . . Good. You're doing just fine." Then to Definitions, then to the story, followed by various exercises. To each section, I allocated a specific amount of time, my eye on the wall clock that hung behind them. This was my punctiliously timed lesson plan, as though I were preparing for the space shuttle liftoff.

It all soon fell apart. I blame it all on Miles.

My plan crumbled with the words for Pronunciation. They were words with the silent *e*, with blended consonants, with the hard and soft *g*, and so forth. Practice pronunciation only with the students, the instructor's manual directed. Don't take time defining them. I tried, but my Bumblebee forced me to violate my conscience. I acquiesced when Miles cut in about one of them. "What does 'quibble' mean?" "Well, ah, let me think," I hesitated. "That means, you know, to sort of . . . ," I was stuck for words. I experimented with an example. "It's like when you argue with someone over some small detail." "I do that all the time with my wife," said Miles. "Is that a quibble?" "No, not really. That's probably a squabble."

I contemplated another example but decided it was worse than the first. "Shucks, let me give you the precise dictionary definition." I quoted from my ever-ready dictionary. "'Quibble' means 'to evade the point of an argument by caviling about words,'" I said. That was like the blind leading the blind. "What does 'caviling' mean?" Miles insisted. He was nothing but persistent about everything. I was in deeper water now. Back to the dictionary. "'Cavil': to raise trivial and frivolous objection." He knew somehow the word "trivial." "But what about 'frivolous'?" he asked.

We were behind schedule and weren't even finished with the words under Pronunciation. I was getting nervous because I wanted to finish the lesson on time. I quickly selected the dictionary's definition: "marked by unbecoming levity." I thought that would end the matter. I should have known better. Now Miles wanted to know what the word "levity" meant. I looked it up and read the definition to myself. "Excessive or unseemly frivolity." I knew that would only bring us back full circle, and Miles would probably interject, "That sounds something like frivolous." "Miles, let's not bother about 'levity,'" I said. "*We're wasting time.* Let's move on."

I tried, I really did try to prevent this mindless squandering of these precious minutes, attempted to reassemble the shattered pieces of my lesson plan and complete the words for Pronunciation. The clock was ticking on. But Chen, his partner in crime, wouldn't let me. She spied the word "slither." I should have told her it was what I wanted to do now—get out of this fumbling attempt at defining words. But she probably knew that already.

It didn't help my predicament by employing one of my foggy illustrations. "Think of a snake sliding back and forth on the ground," I said while looking at the floor, hoping they would imagine that scaled reptile there. "What kind of snake?" Shino asked. I thought my Pool was serious. "Oh, *any kind*. I don't care. Maybe a rattlesnake." "But we don't have rattlesnakes back at my home in Japan," he said. "It doesn't matter if you do or don't," I answered testily. My patience was skating on thin ice. "You know what a snake is like, don't you, and how it moves on the ground?"

Why in the world, I wondered, were Shino and Miles and Chen getting me off the subject at hand. *What's wrong with these Asians?* I thought. They're supposed to be so intelligent. Why can't they concentrate on a single thought for a minute or two?

Miles and Chen said something to each other in Chinese, exchanging knowing glances. Every once in a while, Miles explained something in Chinese to Chen when she was having trouble understanding our English. Then, glancing back at me, he would apologize as he did now. "I'm sorry, Paul. It's not nice to talk our language in front of foreigners." Miles was serious, but I wondered about Shino. "Listen, Shino, come on now. You don't have rattlesnakes back home? Are you pulling my leg?"

I should *never* have asked that. Why in the world I did, I'll never know, for now we were into idioms. We weren't due for idioms till a later lesson. Shino knew what this idiom meant, but the other two didn't. "Pulling one's leg is an idiom. We'll discuss them in a few lessons," I explained, hoping that would close the whole discourse and we could get back to the start.

"What's an idiom?" Chen wanted to know, frustrating my hopes to proceed. "Is it anything like idiot? I heard on television What's-Her-Name call her husband that on *Everybody Loves Raymond*." "I don't have time to watch television," Shino said. "But you should," Chen countered, "that's how you'll learn about American culture." "I don't think 'idiot' is nice word." Miles was getting his two cents' worth in. "I heard someone at the institute call someone else that, and he didn't like it." "The word 'idiot' has *nothing to do* with the word 'idiom,'" I said. *Or did it?* I asked myself. *Maybe I should*

look them up quick in the dictionary. Might they have the same derivation? No,
I decided, *I'm not going to drag this chatter out any further.*

Miles dragged it out. "My wife wanted me to ask you about 'holy moly.'
Lin heard some students at Community College use it. Is that idiom?" "We
have a book on English idioms in Kathy's office," I answered, irritably. "You
can use that book any time you want if you really need to know. But, yes,
you would call it an idiom."

I had, by now, decided to abandon ship. With my lesson plan was so
far off course, I let this rambling talk flow, no matter how unrelated to the
matter at hand. I explained to Miles, "I would say, 'holy, moly' is simply an
exclamation, if you know what the word 'exclamation' means. It's like 'wow.'
Or like 'holy Moses' or 'holy cow.' You hear both of them all the time."

"Who is Moses?" Chen asked. I think she really didn't know. She had
been in the USA for only a few months. And the Bible was certainly not in her
school's curriculum in China. "*Was* Moses. He's dead now," I explained.

"Cows are sacred in India," Shino interjected. "Now that's silly," said
Miles, beginning his first criticism of religion. There would be many more.
"Religion always teaches people wrong things. But not me. I think for myself."
I refused to bite at Miles's bait and get into a theological debate, for which
I'm sure he was aching, or to discuss the sanctity of cows for that matter.
I said, "I first heard that saying from Harry Caray. He was a broadcaster
for the St. Louis Cardinals baseball team and would yell 'holy cow!' after a
great play or if someone hit a home run. Phil Rizzuto used the word all the
time in New York too." Shino knew all about baseball, but the other two
couldn't care less about the sport. And those names Harry Caray and Phil
Rizzuto meant absolutely nothing to all of them. That was fine with me. I
cut short further talk. We went back to the book, skipped Pronunciation,
and salvaged the rest of the period with the next two sections. Of course,
we didn't finish the lesson. My precise lesson plan was shattered.

I don't believe it was their deliberate aim to torpedo my goal for each
hour-and-half class period. I don't even think they collaborated on it. Maybe
Chen and Miles did. But not Shino. At least I didn't think so.

Rather, their irrelevant interruptions sprang up spontaneously and independently like three demonic weeds to corrupt my neat and immaculate garden. There was, however, a common cause at work. They wanted to talk. They wanted to converse. They wanted to practice their English, speak it, not to just passively plod through a lesson, producing prepared answers to the assignment. It was something I wanted them to do—*outside class*, however. I suggested, with words and sayings they had newly learned, "Practice using them *at work*. It doesn't matter if you always get them right. Practice them *there*. That's how you learn."

That's exactly what they wanted to do now, *in class*, and I was blind to see that at first.

And they came at times with questions unrelated to the lesson they wanted to inquire about. Especially Chen. She was intensely interested in learning about our culture, particularly since much of it was new to her. Miles Who-Knows-Everything, who was already five years in the United States, supplied many of the answers before I could. That's why, too, for a spell Chen thought it best if we would discuss newspaper articles about *current* events. She was not a *history* buff. So I clipped them from *USA Today*, the *New York Times*, the *Grand Rapids Press*. Miles predictably volunteered to xerox them. They were articles about abortion, about the elections, about equal pay for women, about poverty in America. After a few weeks of this, however, Chen agreed this approach did not systematically expand their vocabulary. We returned to the book.

Free Medical Advice

They had, perhaps, another reason—unconscious, unintentional—for running us off into tangents. It was the same reason we schemed to maneuver our college's Greek prof into a full-hour bull session—we had not prepared the day's translation assignment!

At any rate, that's what happened to them. They hadn't always completed the exercises, and I could see why. They often arrived for class dead tired. I could see it in their faces. Their research kept them busy frequently, from early morning to late at night. That's why, also, when I offered to drop them off after class at their apartments, Miles, for instance, would decline. This Bumblebee had to buzz straight back to the institute. He had "sacrificed" some mice and had to rush back to his experiment with them. For once, it seemed I caught Miles in a mistake.

"Sacrifice? You mean 'killed,' don't you? Or are you involved in some secret religious ritual in your office?" That last question, I hoped, would tease a friendly sentence or two about religion. "No ritual," he calmly replied. "The animal protection groups don't like word 'kill.' We must always say 'sacrifice.'"

It was agreed, then. And it was unanimous. I got my we-must-finish-the-entire-lesson-on-time obsessiveness under control and announced, "All right. From now on, let's not worry about the time it takes. So what if we get through only half a lesson. Let's do more talking among ourselves—if we feel like it." I thought I heard a collective cheer go up.

I felt like it. I initiated some lessons with open-ended questions to discuss.

I brought my aches and pains and assorted ailments to class for free medical advice. Hypochondriac as I am, some were imagined. Some were real. All were exaggerated. I described them to my three MDs for their remedies, reasoning that would help stimulate a dialogue.

Ever since I retired, I had a problem with sleeping. The problem was not so much about falling asleep. Waking up too early was. My doctor told me that as I get older, I required less sleep. I consulted Shino for answers. "Shino, is that true?" "What happens is that you have inner clock. It controls when you wake up." An inner clock? That was interesting. "Does it tick? Can I turn its hands back?" I wisecracked. Miles scratched his head in disbelief. Chen simply laughed as she always did.

I took my problem to a sleep doctor. I had spent too much time studying downstairs in a darkened room since I retired. "You are not receiving enough sunlight," I learned. I asked Shino if that were so. "Sunlight suppresses melatonin." "Mela—what?" "Melatonin. You need that stored up in your system to keep you asleep. When do you go to bed each night?" "Between eleven thirty and midnight." "Then get up seven hours after you go to bed and go for a walk in sunlight." That meant arising at 7:00 AM. Ugh!

The doctor also had me stay overnight, twice, in a sleep center. I was diagnosed with sleep apnea.

I told you Miles was always prepared to supply his help and advice. Not that the others weren't. But with Miles, it was usually short and snappy, for the immediate present, and that was that, like the Bumblebee he was, flitting quickly from one flower to another.

With Shino, it was different. He was deliberate, thorough, drawing deeply from the pool he was before he presented his well-researched remedy. I received by e-mail a lengthy, detailed report from Shino:

Regarding the sleep apnea. It is also called Pickwickian syndrome that is named after Charles Dickens's novel as follows: "Fat Joe, from Charles Dickens' novel the *Pickwick Papers*, suffered from excessive daytime sleepiness to such an extent that he would fall asleep while knocking on a door." Losing weight, stop drinking before going to bed, and stop smoking (I think you are not a smoker) are the things you have to do. I know you like scotch, but I recommend you not to drink at least four hours before you go to bed. They say that the accident at the nuclear power plant at Three Mile Island and the explosion of the space shuttle *Challenger* were due to common errors caused by this disease. You said that you are using the contraption. Probably you are using a device as below.

Then followed two images: one that displayed the nature of the problem; the other, how to wear the contraption.

The contraption, a mask to cover my nose and mouth, pumped air into these openings. It was a failure. It annoyed me so I couldn't fall asleep, and when I did, I still woke up early. I gave it up and consulted Shino again in class, who told me, "Well then, sleep on your right side." "And not on left side where heart is," Chen added.

I could always count on Shino for the most exhaustive and individualized panacea for whatever ailed me. The best part was it never cost me a cent.

I was genuinely delighted that we had decided to scuttle my original lesson plan. From then on, I diverted at least a half hour into a good old-fashioned "bull session."

Purgatory

An early lesson introduced us to Pearl S. Buck's short story "The Old Demon." I just began the class when Kathy entered the room with the church's new staff member. Mahmud was a Lebanese whose role was to evangelize among refugees from the Near East. Kathy previously informed me about his position and introduced him as such, carefully avoiding the word "evangelize."

He was missionary minded, I could tell, with an eager-beaver look in his eyes for converts among the class. He took his time getting acquainted with the class, going carefully over their names, as though preparing a list for future prospects. I sensed a disaster in the making. Was he laying the groundwork, I worried, for assuming control of the class eventually, and would my friends suspect this was the church's plan all the while: *conversion?* It wasn't, of course, but how were they to know? I was annoyed by the time he leisurely took away from the class session—I was still trying to overcome my let's-finish-this-lesson-on-time obsessiveness—but more concerned that the class would lose confidence in my intention to help with their English and defect from the program.

But Chen's comment solidified my sole ownership of the class and helped to establish a bond between them and me. "I want to say something nice about Paul. He always speaks clearly and slowly. That helps a lot." She was irritated, saying in effect, "Let's get on with the class." Kathy and Mahmud took the hint, exited, and we returned to Pearl Buck.

Notice she called me Paul. They, all of them, called me Paul—not pastor; not reverend, as I was known around the church; not professor, my title throughout thirty-four years of teaching college students (and other assorted nicknames assigned by students)—but Paul. Initially this was a shock to my sense of self-importance, my dignity. In reality, nothing more signified what I intended for our relationship. It sounds corny, I know, but I did not want to be their teacher and they my students. We were to be friends, I hoped, on a first-name basis, collaborating on a joint adventure.

"The Old Demon" in Pearl Buck's story is a river in China. The main character is old Mrs. Wang. As always with the story section of the lesson, the three took turns reading out loud a portion of it. "Shall I correct you if you mispronounce a word?" I asked. "Yeah, sure," said Chen. I hated to do that because I did not want to embarrass them. So I allowed some errors to slip in during the first lesson or two. That was another mistake of mine.

Pronunciation was important to them—they reported orally on their research before groups at the institute—and they were not embarrassed if I corrected them. They welcomed it, really. None of them had a heavy accent. Few corrections were required, except when "staring" came out "starring," "gazed" sounded more like "gaused," and "purgatory" became "purge-atory."

The Japanese attacked the Chinese in the story, bombarded Mrs. Wang's village to be specific. Japan and China had their past conflicts and even some present tensions. I was curious to see if any critical comments would be exchanged between the two Chinese and Shino. There were none. But the mention of war opened the door for Miles to deliver one of his knows-everything's. He presented a short history of China's troubles with Japan. He concluded by mentioning that in 1937, two hundred thousand Japanese troops were stationed in China. They massacred forty-two thousand civilians, he indicated, mostly women and children. He claimed that something like twenty thousand cases of rape occurred. Surprisingly, there was no bitterness in Miles's report. He even went on to say that some atrocities may have been committed by Chinese communists. He was trying to be fair while simultaneously criticizing communist leaders, past and present.

My Swan remained silent during this recital of Sino-Japanese conflicts. No defensive waves disturbed the surface of my Pool. We all knew what was transpiring here. Miles was just being Miles Who-Knows-Everything, just trying to impress.

Purgatory. The word appeared in Buck's story of Mrs. Wang's kinship with her husband. "He, poor man, had been drowned in a flood when he was still young. And it had taken her years to get him prayed out of Buddhist purgatory."

"Do you know what the word stands for—'purgatory'?" I asked.

"'Purge' means 'to clean out dirt,' or something like that," Shino responded.

"Right," I said, "but I mean 'purgatory.' Do Buddhists teach about a purgatory?" I had read a short book about Buddhism years ago, but I couldn't remember much about its teaching. I really wanted to know.

"I do know Buddhists have temples," I said. "Yes, people go there all time to pray for good luck," Miles said mockingly. He evaluated all religions with equal sarcasm since he believed in none of them.

Chen equated purgatory with hell. "It's where bad people go." "How bad do you have to be?" I egged her on. "There are eighteen stories in hell," she claimed. "The badder you are, lower you go." Since she said this with a smile, I smiled back when I asked, "Is there something like an elevator in hell to get you to the top, to get out?" I did not receive a clear answer.

I realized that all the information I received from them about their religion, their politics, whatever it was about their culture had to be filtered through their popular misconceptions. I took Chen's eighteen stories in hell with a grain of salt. I recalled how many ill-informed Christians misrepresent their faith by talking off the top of their heads.

"What about Christians?" Miles asked. "Do you have purgatory?" "Well, I don't, but some Christian groups teach that there is a purgatory."

"Do you do bad things?" Chen challenged me. She was needling me. We were developing a congenial relationship.

"Certainly I do. Not only bad things. I think bad thoughts. Say bad things."

"Then where do you go? How many stories down?"

"I have an elevator—Jesus. He gets me out of the hole I'm in. He gets me to the top—to God as my father."

Blank looks accompanied an awkward pause. It seemed they weren't quite sure what I meant.

Miles broke the silence, "I just believe in being real good person, doing good things for people."

I determined I'd try to get inside that idea and see where it would lead us. I asked, "But why? Why do good?"

"Because that's right way. I need to help people."

"I'm sure you do, Miles. I know you do. But I wonder why. Why do good in the first place?"

"There's so much suffering in world. I use science to help."

"Science doesn't tell you why you help. It's only a tool, isn't it? You can use science to make a bomb to kill people or find a cure for cancer. It's a tool you use to help. But why help?"

"I don't know why. It's not because of god, though. I don't even know if there is god—or two or three of them. Something just tells me to do good. And it's not because of religion either. Not because of heaven or hell or purgatory. I don't know what happens after death."

"Does something ever tell you to do bad? Something tells me that."

"Sure. And I do it sometimes. But I don't like it. That's why, I guess. That's why I try to do good. It makes me feel better than when I do bad."

"Aren't we all like that, Miles? Even Chen." She frowned. "Sorry about that, Chen, just kidding," I said, glancing at her to my side. She laughed.

"I guess that's way it works," Miles summed things up. "Bad things hurt. Good things make me feel good. They help people. They make me feel good inside. There is some selfishness."

Obviously, Miles had done some thinking on this subject. But it did not budge him one inch closer to consider religion—any religion.

Shino reintroduced purgatory. He had been silent since he first defined "purge." Of the three, he was the most informed, more knowledgeable, and by far more inquisitive about Christianity. My Pool drew from his depth.

"Catholics have a teaching about purgatory. It's where they go after they die to purge themselves before they appear before God. Anyway, that's what I've learned. Am I correct, Paul?"

I suggested my own tentative qualified understanding of contemporary Roman Catholic teaching, prefacing it with, "Now, I don't really know for sure, but . . ."

The hour was drawing to a close. Mike, his class over, passed by our room. "There's Mike," I said." "He's a Roman Catholic. Let's ask him."

Mike seemed somewhat indifferent about the subject. Perhaps he had not been well informed about the teaching.

Chen was getting up from her seat, preparing to leave with the others. Chen, ever curious about our culture, said, "I would like to know more about this purgatory. Would you two come to my apartment to talk?"

"Absolutely. When?"

"Next Tuesday? Say around seven?"

"Fine. See you then."

Chen started for the doorway. With her back to me, moving away, she was addressing me when she said, "Just don't try to make a Christian out of me." I replied, "And don't you try to make a Buddhist out of me." Let me tell you, that was an incredibly inappropriate comment for me to make. I guess it just sort of slipped out. Gliding through the doorway, she turned, looked at me, and her broad smile absolved my unwarranted snappy comeback. We were still friends.

Yes, But

Chen was a gracious hostess. There were some grapes on a table, other Chinese delicacies, and tea—jasmine tea—served in little cups.

When Mike and I entered, we noticed Chen in slippers, her shoes set neatly by the side of the doorway. "Shall we take off our shoes?" Mike offered. "No no no. Not necessary. Just come in."

It was a modest apartment, with a kitchenette off the living room and, presumably, a bedroom and bathroom around the corner from the kitchenette. Many of the scientists lived in one of two apartment buildings. They were set at right angles from each other, off Prospect Avenue, three or four blocks east of the institute. They were two-story buildings with perhaps eight or ten apartments in each. A minioval swimming pool separated the two buildings. It was never filled with water, as far as I could tell, with dead leaves and debris settled at the bottom. Pointing to it through the living room window, I joked, "Be careful about taking a midnight dip into it. Make sure there's water in it first." Chen smiled. "We never use it."

Shino, Miles, and his wife, Lin, lived in the other building. Soon after we entered, there was a short knock on the door, and Shino entered, having also been invited. He took his seat on a short couch, with a book in his hand. I sat next to him. "Look what I have," Shino said. "What's that?" "A Bible." Shino opened it to John's Gospel. Chen was busy talking to Mike.

My word, I thought. Did Shino want to discuss John's Gospel? I doubted Chen intended that with her "just don't try to make a Christian out of me" still ringing in my ears. An informal discussion about purgatory was planned, not some discourse about the life of Christ. I was cautious about delving into the subject. So I asked some neutral questions.

"Where did you get that?" "I once attended scientific conference in England, at Liverpool. Another scientist gave it to me. He was Baptist. He lives in Indiana now. I visited him when I first came to America."

I was tempted to define the differences between Baptists and Lutherans, but squelched the urge. This was not the time to discuss denominational disagreements. "Have you read any of John's Gospel? Of all the Gospels, it's the easiest to read." "A little," he said. "Just first paragraphs. But it's hard to understand." The concepts, the ideas he meant, not the English. "Want to talk about it sometime?" I suggested. Getting up from his seat, he said, "I have so little time." I left it at that.

This was my feeble and failed stab at ushering in Christianity by the side door.

Meanwhile, Chen had taken Mike to a large map of China fastened on the wall. I joined them. She was singing the praises of her homeland. "Look, there's Shanghai, my home, such a beautiful city. There are over three thousand skyscrapers in it." Then the Yangtze River, she pointed out, the limestone forests, the snow-frosted mountains, the Great Wall of China, the Himalayas. She was in her glory. I initially suspected that she was making an odious comparison between China's landscape and ours. But she wasn't, really. She was only doing what we all do—exalting with pride in her own country.

Mike was better than I was in showing his respect for Chen's portrayal of China. I had to resist a counterattack with a voice within me, which was preparing a "yes, but." Yes, *Shanghai is beautiful you say,* but *have you ever seen San Francisco?* I had a hard time keeping my lips sealed. One reason I had joined ESL was the same reason Van Andel welcomed foreign scientists—to help smooth international relationships. I was not always great at it. I would not make a very good foreign diplomat.

"Remember, things are different—not better," Mike Kosswig had warned me. Mike Kosswig was a German, seven or eight years older than I, and had come to America in the 1950s. He worked for a large chemical company in St. Louis where he had joined my father's parish. It was 1955, and I was a seminary student. He became a friend of our family and joined us on Christmas Day afternoon. He was lying on our living room floor with a map of Europe spread out before him. He planned to visit his aged mother and two sisters in Berlin. Since he had never traveled in Europe outside Germany, he was designing an extensive tour of Europe for next summer. Looking up from his map at me, he asked, "Why don't you come with me?" I looked at my father, then my mother. "Why not?" they said.

Before we left on our tour, Mike cautioned, "When you experience everything in Europe, don't compare. Say to yourself, 'It's different in America, not better.'"

It was a life-changing event for me. I still have the postcards I sent to my folks, which they kept for me. I waxed enthusiastically in them about everything in Europe. The Champs-Élysées and Louvre in Paris. The mountains of Switzerland and Southern Germany. The charm of their little villages. The majesty of their soaring cathedrals. The Tivoli park of Copenhagen. Princess Street in Edinburgh. Dublin, where I sipped the incomparable Irish coffee, a gift from a resident I met there. The Tower of London where Anne Boleyn lost her head. All that history. All the Europeans who welcomed this young American. Don't forget, these were the Europeans of fifty years ago, long before the Iraq War.

Few of us students toured Europe in those days. Filled with myself when I returned, I haughtily explained to my classmates that here and there, with this and that, it was better in Europe than in America.

It was easier for me to admit that then. I was "showing off" to my stay-at-home fellow Americans. Little did I know then that I would marry a German ten years later. Or that I would have foreigners on my own turf making comparisons. That was harder to accept. And that's when the juices of my "yes, but" came to a boil.

Listen to Miles. "We respect old age in China more than you do here." "How so?" I challenged. "We always ask old, retired president at our institute for his advice before we make decisions." "What if he is wrong?" "Doesn't matter. We respect old age in China." "*Yes, but,*" I wanted to reply, but didn't. "You don't enjoy the freedoms we have."

Then Shino. "We don't have level of poverty in Japan as here." Yes, but *you have a homogenous society. You don't welcome poor immigrants as we do.*

Now Chen, with her "Shanghai, so beautiful." Yes, but *think of the pollution in it.* There was even, or especially, Gertraud. The clean streets, the museums, the free-flowing, glorious beer and wine, whatever else it was in Germany with which she made odious comparisons. In each case, except for my wife, of course, I resisted the "yes, but."

If my foreign friends learned some English from me, I learned something else from them—to gulp down this overbearing nationalistic pride. Must everything be "better" *here?* Can't I swallow for once the fact that something is "better" *there?* Some small steps forward to fostering international goodwill can be made if one avoids the "yes, but."

Chen was in love with China. You could see that. You could feel her heart back in Shanghai, with her parents, her husband, and young son. It made me think and made me humble. There are others, after all—oceans far off—deeply devoted to their homeland and family, as we are to ours. We have that all in common—a universal trait—and what a pity, I thought, that the folly of chauvinistic nationalistic pride should ever put our nations at serious odds with each other.

That was this evening's lesson. When Mike and I spoke our "thank-yous" and "good-bye's," I left with more sympathy and understanding for this young lady, with a strengthened friendship with my Swan.

Incidentally, purgatory—the word—never came up.

A Near Disaster

After the aborted analysis of purgatory in Chen's apartment, I wondered if Chen was reluctant to discuss religion in the first place. Perhaps it would be less intimidating for them if we moved our classes from the parlors, the basement beneath the church's sanctuary, to a more neutral site. I suggested to Mike the institute itself. Their natural surroundings would make them all feel at ease. Mike thought otherwise and said that "they would rather want to escape their workplace and would prefer a break from it." He was correct, of course.

The only other alternative was the classrooms of the church's parochial school attached to the church building. We decided to move our meeting up two flights of stairs, up another short set of stairs, and down a long hallway with classrooms on the left. It was more cheery there. The windows looked out on to the parking lot, which separated the church from the institute. We awaited our students for the next class session.

My trio did not arrive as a group because they did not work as a group. They researched in separate labs and offices. If one or the other was detained, or on rare occasions had to cancel because of some last-minute delays, the others would be informed and carry the news back to me. They were a considerate bunch. They showed up one by one usually, and this time Miles was the first. I greeted him at the entrance, where we awaited the other two. He was in an exuberant mood, lifted by some success in a complex project. He reported it to me in technical terms, which I did not understand. I could tell he was in a take-charge mode.

When Chen and Shino appeared, I ushered them down the hallway and into the sixth-grade classroom. There were small desks in it with chairs set upside down on top of them to facilitate the custodian's mopping up underneath. We needed to rearrange four of them for our group.

My Bumblebee flew into action. It was springtime, and Miles opened some windows and turned on a fan. "Is this OK, Paul? Don't we need some fresh air?" he asked without waiting for an answer. He removed the chairs from the desks and put them on the floor. "Here, Chen, you sit in center," Miles said as he started to arrange a little semicircle. Shino was directed to sit off to the left. "I'll sit here," Miles said, positioning him to the right. "Paul, you should sit here in front of us." You'd think he was the CEO of Microsoft preparing for a meeting of the board.

I didn't have to lift a finger. Miles did all the work. It was Miles again, hurrying around to prepare for the class.

Had I seated them taking into account their political persuasions vis-à-vis China's government authorities, I would have placed Shino in the center, separating the other two from each other, Chen to the far right, Miles to the far left. They had two conflicting convictions about China's bureaucrats.

We had not gotten to the exercises for the last lesson, Pearl Buck's "The Old Demon." We returned to them. The first set of exercises began with Understanding the Story. It contained a series of incomplete sentences to which they were to select one of four answers. The first sentence began, "The war is not a reality to the villagers because . . ." Shino and Miles chose correctly. "It has not yet affected their lives."

But Chen chose "Buddhists are a peace-loving people." Miles detected an opening here to criticize religion. "It's religion that causes so many wars. That's trouble with it." I wanted to respond, "Not religion, but bad religion." But I ignored the criticism.

Another sentence began, "Mrs. Wang had decided not to pay for the removal of her husband's hand from purgatory because . . ." Shino selected the correct answer, "Had more pressing need for money." And he began to inquire about purgatory. We didn't need that now, and so I quickly turned to Miles. "What did you choose?" Conditioned by his antireligious sentiment, he chose "She was angered by the priest's greediness." Miles said, "You always have to pay them before they will pray for you." Chen, however, complained, "Well, I got it wrong again. I thought it was 'She did not have the money.'"

Chen frowned and dropped her eyes to her book. Disheartened by her repeated failures to comprehend the English language, she asked, "By way, at what level of English is this book for, at high school here in America I mean." I said that Kathy told me for those in early high school, say tenth grade or so. "Then I'd never be able to attend college here." "You thinking of taking a course somewhere?" I asked. "No, no, I'm just thinking I'd never make it here if I tried."

"Sure you would. You're so intelligent, you'd catch on fast. In fact, I wonder why you're all taking this course in the first place. You seem to be able to communicate in English well enough." "But so much of the scientific literature is in English, polished English," Shino said, "and conferences around world are usually in English. We need to get better at it." "Besides," added Miles, "we need to expand our vocabulary. There are so many words I don't know."

"That's exactly my problem," Chen complained again. "I'd never understand lecture in college well enough." I said, "But other students would help you before a test. They would. Maybe even the prof would, in some small classes at least. I did that with two foreign students I had in class. Both were young females. I can't remember the name of the one, but Hagiwara was the other one."

"That's Japanese name," Shino noticed. "What course was she taking?" "In religion, one in the New Testament," I said. "Why religion?" Shino asked. "There are so few Christians in Japan. Was she one?"

"I helped Hagiwara prepare for a test, and we conversed for an hour," I went on, "and the way she talked, I suspected she was. So I asked her. It happened her whole family was Christian, going even back to her grandparents, she told me. They heard the Gospel from a Methodist missionary. I even asked her if she was glad to be a Christian. I could see her face glow with joy. I asked her, 'But isn't it hard being a Christian in Japan? Do you ever get persecuted?' 'Not in physical way,' she admitted. 'But you do feel it, way people act toward you.' 'You mean you get ostracized?'"

"What does 'ostracized' mean?" Chen broke in.

Miles explained, "It's related to word 'ostrich.' That is bird who hides its head in sand to not being seen when chased."

"Well, sort of," I said, trying not to be too corrective. "She wasn't hiding her Christianity. She was happy to be one. It's rather that she sometimes felt excluded from society."

The Hagiwara story was my attempt to introduce Christianity in an indirect way. Maybe it would pique their curiosity and lead to some inquiries. Miles was unimpressed. Shino was on the verge of probing into the subject. So was Chen, I sensed, but she quickly caught herself and avoided the issue with, "See what I mean? I just don't know those kinds of words. I need to learn more English."

I always kept our classroom door open. There were fifteen minutes or so left in our period. Out of the corner of my eye, while we were still talking, I caught the figure of a man standing in the doorway. He motioned to me, and whatever he wanted, I resisted the interruption and concluded he could wait for a few minutes. I ignored him.

Five minutes later, he reappeared. It was Mahmud, our Lebanese evangelist. This time he entered the room and approached me. Silently he handed me a note and exited. The gist of the note was this: I was to leave the class and join Mike in his classroom while my three remained behind, waiting. Mike's class was to join mine, and Mahmud and I were to meet with Mike. I wondered what was up.

Reluctantly, I excused myself, and when I sat with Mike, Mahmud provided us with these instructions. Mike and I were to meet as usual with our classes for the next two weeks. Thereafter, he would jointly meet alone with the two classes. We were to be excused from our duties. He planned a social hour with them for two sessions. Refreshments will be served while he bonded with them. They would have a grand time. It was clear he was going to "soften" them up. For he planned to conduct several formal classes during the following weeks to discuss Christianity. His aim was obvious: *conversion.*

Astonished, Mike and I looked at each other in utter disbelief. We were floored! We started to object, stuttering what to say, "But . . . but . . ."

Mahmud said, "Don't worry. This will work. I know what I'm doing." Abruptly he stood up and left us, turning at the doorway to deliver us a reassuring smile. He was gone in a flash to announce the altered arrangements to our two classes.

Mahmud was an enthusiastic, dedicated, well-intentioned crusader for Christ—and hopelessly naive. What was he imagining? we thought to ourselves. Was this any way to introduce them to Christ? Did he think they would welcome this invasion of their busy schedules with several hours of chitchat over potato chips, pretzels, and punch? Worse, did he really think they would want to consider the Christian religion in favor of their, and the church's, stated desire to improve their English? The dear man's hope was simpleminded, akin to thinking one could create a capitalist out of Mao Tse-Tung over tea and cookies, or Martin Luther an atheist after a glass of German beer.

Two classrooms down the hallway, we heard his voice—the rest were as silent as death—make his proposal to his "prospects." For the next few minutes, we had the funny feeling that this was the calm before the storm.

We slipped out the back door and hurried to the parking lot to intercept the group before they returned to the institute. The storm had broken. Infuriated, Miles was already striding angrily out of the parking lot like a jet with fumes trailing behind him. My Pool, composed and self-controlled as usual, was mildly agitated, assuming understandably that some mistake had been made and would be rectified. My Swan's feathers were all aflutter, perplexed and irritated like the rest of Mike's class.

We immediately quieted the brewing tempest. "A terrible mistake had been made," we reassured them. "Nothing will change. ESL will continue as before."

The next day, Kathy, informed of the previous evening's near calamity, instructed Mahmud never ever again to inject himself in our ESL classes.

For the next several sessions, I gingerly walked around the subject of religion, bearing Miles particularly in mind. I was resolved to avoid the impression that the ESL program was a disguised scheme designed to convert them.

A Pizza Party with Politics

"What do you want on your pizza?" I asked my friends. "I love pizza," answered Shino. "We have Pizza Huts all over Japan." "You do? I didn't realize that." "Not only Pizza Huts. We have McDonald's, Burger Kings, Subways, Wendy's, and Kentucky Fried Chicken places."

Miles informed us that in China, "We have only McDonald's, Kentucky Fried Chicken, and Pizza Hut." "I hope you don't eat too much of that greasy stuff here," I warned. "It's loaded with calories. You'll get fat." Miles confessed that he and Lin ate at McDonald's. "But only on special occasions," he explained, "when we celebrate something like anniversary."

"Anyway," I repeated, "what do you like on your pizza? pepperoni? sausage? anchovies?" Gertraud and I had planned a pizza party at our place. She had never met them. And I was taking orders as we began our class. We intended to have a fun time with them, to visit informally and get to know each other in a casual setting. "You can let your hair down and relax from your research. And, Miles, Lin is also invited."

"What was that," detected Shino, "another idiom?" I answered, "What do you mean? Let your hair down? Well, yeah, that's an idiom. It simply means to act freely, naturally, informally."

"I can't eat pizza," Miles said. "Why not?" "I'm allergic to cheese. But that's OK. I don't have to eat anything. Besides, we'll all bring something, won't we?" Miles suggested, involving the others as he looked at them, though it sounded more like an order. "You don't have to bring anything. Just bring yourselves," I insisted.

"You don't know how to get to our place," I remembered. "Here. I'll write down the directions." Before I could put pen to paper, Miles volunteered, "Don't bother. I'll get directions off computer. I'll drive."

"Wait a minute. I almost forgot. What do you like to drink? Do you all drink beer or wine or scotch?" Shino's face brightened at the mention of scotch.

"I don't drink anything alcoholic," Miles announced. I admired his restraint. *He's so careful about his health*, I thought. I just had to tease him. "Why not? Is it against your religion?" "Religion?" Miles laughed. "You're kidding. It's just that I'm allergic to alcohol. I'll pass out if I drink it." "You have to drink something. What about soda?" "I drink Coke. But don't go to any trouble. I can drink water. Lin will do same." "We'll get some Coke," I said.

This was Miles again, not wishing to be a bother while simultaneously taking command of the arrangements. Only this time Miles committed one breach in etiquette. He took the liberty of inviting two others, Dong Kong and his Spanish girlfriend. They were scheduled to transfer to the cancer clinic in New York City next week. They were coming in another car.

On his way, Miles called from his car on his cell phone. Shino had advised him, "Miles, you just don't invite other people without telling Paul ahead of time."

"Paul, I'm sorry. I'm so sorry. I also invited Dong Kong and his friend," he called. "That's OK, Miles. Just forget about it."

At the door, Miles was full of apologies again. "I should have known better. I didn't think. But they are already on their way."

"I told you to forget about it, Miles," I told him as I opened wide our entrance. I gave him a reassuring big kiss on his full, round cheek. "The more's the merrier. Just come in."

Chen entered and presented Gertraud with a colorful embroidered emblem. It still hangs on our doorway wall leading to our bedroom. This was the first of the many gifts these Asians always brought when invited for an evening.

Our place is a modest condo, but Chen, thinking of their cramped living quarters back home, was amazed. "Just look at this," she said. "So much space!" My Swan swiftly glided through a short hallway, through the dining and living rooms, straight for the entrance to the deck. Excited, she opened wide the glass and screen doors, an unwitting invitation for potential mosquitoes and flies. Gertraud, quick as a cat, shut the screen door behind her. (Gertraud considers it a mortal sin to leave doors open for uninvited assorted bugs.) Chen stood on the deck and took in the stretch of lawn and woods beyond. "I'd just love to live in a place like this," she said. I could not have guessed at the time that she would one day turn that desire into a reality.

Meanwhile, Miles, Lin, Shino, and I were gathered in the family room just off the kitchen. Miles, feeling fully at home by now, was pontificating about something or another. Lin stood off behind him and rolled her eyes, silently spoofing her husband, the man Who-Knows-Everything. She placed a bottle of wine on the counter, which separated the family room from the kitchen. "This is for rest of you," Shino said as he set down a tray of noodles he prepared. I soon devoured half of it. When Gertraud asked for the recipe, Shino replied, "I'll show you how to make it."

Fifteen minutes later, Dong Kong and his Spanish girl friend arrived—I still cannot recall her name. We were all milling around in separate rooms. This was to be an easygoing, pleasant party, enjoying each other's company. The only fly in the ointment was that the war in Iraq was firing up.

Gertraud was in the living room with Dong Kong and his friend. Gertraud and I had conflicting views of the war, and she made them known to the two, who agreed with her. She was against all wars, having grown up in Germany during World War II and had experienced the ravages of war. She was against the war in Iraq. She was opposed to the war in Afghanistan. She was even opposed to the Gulf War. I think she even had cast her absentee ballot against the War of 1812 and the French-Indian War. She was not exactly enamored of President Bush.

After some time and some pizza, Dong Kong, the Spaniard, and Gertraud joined me and the others in the family room. The evening was drawing to its close. Dong's friend sat opposite me. She looked squarely at me, her dark eyes flashing. I could see she was spoiling for a fight over the war.

In order to skirt an impending clash, I posed an innocent question for her. "How long do you think before the cure for cancer will be found?" "Maybe in two hundred years. Maybe never," she snapped at me.

Then she started railing against the USA. She let loose a litany of complaints.

We are wrong about capital punishment.

We are wrong to ever oppose abortion.

We are responsible for global warming.

We are ruining the environment.

We are treating our allies like subordinates.

Then came her salvo about Iraq.

"We have trouble with the Basques in Spain. But we don't just drop a bomb on them!" She then dropped her own bomb. With utter disdain, she said, "You Americans!"

There was deathlike silence. My Asians were embarrassed for me and held their tongues.

Chen quickly left for the bathroom.

Shino gulped and took a swig from his scotch.

Lin poked Miles in his ribs, a hint to change the subject. Miles resisted and kept quiet for once.

Gertraud feared an outbreak of hostilities. What would Paul say?

Paul said nothing.

After I quieted my annoyance at this attack from an uninvited guest, an invasive encroachment on our heretofore sociable atmosphere and from a foreigner at that, I recalled a joke.

"Dave Barry, the humorist, once jested about the European wars many centuries ago," I began. "It went something like this. 'England declared war on Spain. Spain simultaneously declared war on France, while France declared war on England. Then England, by mistake, declared war on itself.'"

Even my antagonist laughed. An uneasy armistice prevailed.

Later that night, I reflected on the evening. You had classic Oriental courtesy, an angry Spaniard, a critical German, a defensive American all in the mix. What a clash of cultures. A microcosm of the world scene.

Chen Wins

Of the three, Chen entertained the most anti-Americanism—at least during her initial months here. It did not emerge from below, tsunami-like, and swamp us with mean-spirited criticism. It was more of an undercurrent, tempered by traditional Oriental courtesy. It surfaced on occasion like a ripple with insinuating questions, implied complaints, subtle disparagements of our foreign policies. It welled up especially when it involved her traffic violations.

Chen purchased an auto—foreign made, of course, a used Japanese Toyota—when she arrived in Grand Rapids. She needed to travel and "learn the culture" as she said. She had distant relatives in Chicago and visited them at times, taking in a museum or two. They were "interesting" museums, never described in more superlative terms than that.

On one occasion when I was her passenger, I wanted to point out that there were speed limits posted, which were intended to encourage her compliance. I assumed she would notice in time the disparity between the figures on her speedometer and those posted, though the latter she seemed to regard as a mere request. It was a harbinger of things to come. When, however, she treated a stop sign with indifference, as though it were a hostile intruder, I advised she might want to accord such directives with a little more than an aloof disinterest.

"What does 'aloof' mean?"

I explained.

"I see." She smiled. "I'll try to remember that." Evidently, she didn't try hard enough.

Her first encounter with the cruel American justice system was when she drove with Shino to a football game at Michigan State University. She approached the stadium on the inner lane of a major four-lane thoroughfare. Having missed an earlier exit to the stadium parking lot, she was inwardly moved to take a sharp U-turn at an intersection and sped off in the opposite direction. She assumed, supposedly, that the police nearby in a McDonald's parking lot were for the sole purpose of apprehending hardened criminals, drug dealers, and pedophiles, and would ignore her innocent maneuver. They did not.

It was the most unfair thing in the world that they ticketed her. She murmured something about picking on a foreigner. "Now now, Chen, how could they have known you were a foreigner?" "They just did, that's all." It was something like a woman's intuition, China made, I guess.

"I make U-turns on Prospect where I live. And you can make them in China." "You *may* in America," I said, correcting her grammar, "but not on a four-lane thoroughfare in front of oncoming traffic." "And if you must," I added, "it's best not to do that smack under the noses of the cops." She detected the wisdom in my warning and vowed to swear off U-turns in the USA.

The fine was, of course, also unjustly excessive. To help repair her image of the American justice system, I sympathized with her. I suggested she appeal the fine, though I questioned the worth in the long run of an eighty-mile round-trip to the court and back.

"The least you could do is to ask them to reduce the fine," I suggested. "Really? Do you think I should? Go to court?" she said, timidly.

"Why not? What do you have to lose? Play on their sympathies as a newcomer to our country. You're a recent arrival. You're just learning the ropes. Tell them you're sorry. You didn't realize a U-turn was so bad. Tell the court that. Maybe they will even forgive the fine."

Fired by the urge to remove any blemish on the good name of a Chinese, she revved up her resolve to appeal. Still smarting by her perceived assault on a foreigner, she drove the forty miles to the court near the university where her transgression was recorded.

Her American friends at Van Andel coached her on how to phrase her appeal. She memorized it, turned on her Oriental charm, and suggested that "perhaps, just perhaps, a $90 fine was too much and might be reduced, if it pleased the court, to something like $50."

The next day she called me. She trumpeted her triumph. "I won!"

"What happened? What did they do?" I asked. "They reduced fine." "To what?" "To $70."

"But, Chen, you saved only $20. Was it worth the expense of the trip, the gas, the time away from work and all that?"

"So what," she said. There was a principle at work here, I was given to understand. *Such a tiny victory*, I thought. It didn't matter. She had gotten the upper hand. The system worked after all—her system.

The score: Chen, 1; USA, 0.

Tie Score

Chen's second traffic violation was more serious and potentially fatal. It was winter, and the interstate was tricky driving on her way home from the university. She went there from time to time to collaborate with some scientists on a cancer research project.

We were out of town at the time and learned about her accident on our return when Gertraud answered the phone. After the initial exchange of pleasantries, I heard from the adjoining room Gertraud exclaim, "My word, you could have been killed." Chen detailed the whole episode to Gertraud and then told her, "Here's Paul, tell him about it," handing me the phone. "It wasn't my fault!" She was adamant about it. I could hear the fire in her voice. Inspired by her first triumphant appearance, she was prepared to take it to court. Here we go again.

It seems she was in the left-hand lane preparing to pass a semi. Someone on the right cut in front of her, bent on being the first to pass the semi. She slammed on her brakes, lost control on the accumulated slush, and careened into the rear of the semi. Her car was totaled. "Were you injured?" "No. Not at all." She had emerged unscathed. What suffered was the injustice inflicted. "How can I be at fault?" Her protest seemed reasonable, considering her account of the "facts." I suspected she had challenged the speed limit again. But I hesitated to introduce that possibility as a contributing factor.

Next Monday, an e-mail arrived: "Dear Paul, would you have time on Wednesday to drive me to court at St. Johns?" She was scheduled to make her appearance at 9:00 AM. At 9:00 AM? I totaled up the miles and estimated the hour we would have to depart. Eleven miles westward to her apartment, back to our place, and then east for another forty or so. That meant the sound of the alarm at 6:00 AM. Ouch!

I e-mailed these arrangements: "I will pick you up on Tuesday after work, and you could stay overnight at our place. That will spare us time the next morning. Is this OK?"

She promptly e-mailed: "That's great with me if it's all right with you. Thanks."

We ate supper and visited a bit before retiring. She rehearsed for us her defense. I jokingly suggested that her case could be advanced if she appeared at court wearing a clerical collar. "A clerical collar? What's that?" "You've seen them, Chen. On Roman Catholic priests. That white band attached to a black shirt. It indicates their profession. Some Protestant ministers wear them too." I hesitated if I should add this but did anyway, "It can help smooth the way out of some predicament." "How? Did it you?" she asked. I admitted it once gave me some preferential treatment. Since she was interested in how, I told her my story. "This is what actually happened, Chen.

"When we lived in New York, I was late at night returning from a meeting in Queens. I was on the Van Wyck Expressway on my way home north to Westchester County. Somehow I got confused and turned off the Van Wyck Expressway on to the Long Island Expressway heading west straight for Manhattan. There was no stopping now, and a U-turn was impossible, if not illegal. [She remembered how U-turns can get one into trouble.] I screeched to a dead stop a hundred feet from the toll booth leading through the East River and into Manhattan—which was the last place I wanted to be. I hated driving in the Big Apple. I avoided it whenever I could. I'd get lost for sure. No telling when I'd get home.

"'What's the problem, Father?' asked a sympathetic policeman, noticing my clerical collar. His Irish brogue betrayed him. A Roman Catholic cop no doubt. He'd make an exception, I hoped, and get me turned around."

"Father?" wondered Chen. "What was that? Why father?"

"That's what people call a Roman Catholic priest." "Did you tell him you weren't one of them?" She wasn't asking. She was accusing. "This was not the time for fine distinctions," I explained. "Besides, I wasn't lying. I was circumventing the truth."

I went on, "'No problem,' said the policeman. He removed the orange cones that separated the westbound from the east on the Long Island Expressway, which were joined at the toll. I made the officially blessed U-turn. 'Get home safely, Father. And drive carefully.'" I was a little embarrassed to admit how a clerical collar could provide preferential treatment, denied others, and helped bypass other irregularities from time to time in my experience. Chen made a mental entry in her record of American favors dispensed to an elite few.

We were up early the next morning. Chen ate two pieces of toast—that's all she wanted. We gulped some coffee—we had no jasmine tea—while I ate my customary oatmeal over a sliced banana. The interstate was a mile from our condo. We were on the interstate in a few minutes. I got our Passat up to seventy miles an hour, the limit. I wanted to push it to eighty to match the cars sweeping by. But I felt Chen's eyes on the speedometer. I suspected she was gathering evidence against me to retaliate for my earlier critique of her traffic violations. Or maybe I'm a little paranoid.

We passed the scene on the left, about where she estimated her accident occurred. That provoked her to chatter aloud her defense once again, which she had been, till then, silently rehearsing. "No trooper saw accident. Why did he believe other witnesses? I wasn't guilty one. Besides, road was slippery."

It was a nervous chatter. I wondered why. "Realize, Paul, in China when you are called before court, you can be in real trouble, serious punishment. It's not how my colleagues at Van Andel describe courts here." This was her first—and only—admission of some defect in China.

Five minutes later, she retreated from her claim about the courts in China and went on the offensive. She remembered the whole clerical collar business. "But isn't it little wrong for you to use your clerical collar to avoid trouble?" She meant 'hypocritical' but didn't know the word.

I avoided her criticism with, "The collar doesn't *always* impress police." Then I told her why. I took her back to New York when I taught at Concordia College. "There is an old chapel—the small original one—at the West Point Military Academy adjoined to the cemetery where army heroes are buried. The

Lutheran cadets and faculty officers used it for Sunday-morning worship. We laughingly referred to it as the dead center of Lutheranism," I told her. (She didn't get the joke.) "The chaplain had retired, and I filled in on Sundays."

"The parkway on the last leg to West Point was hilly, curvy, and usually well patrolled by the state police. Since I was a little late that morning, I put a heavy foot on the accelerator. Surely no police would be watching on this early Sunday morning. One of them was. He ushered me off to the shoulder of the parkway. My overcoat covered my clerical collar—it was winter—and I opened it wide so as to make it conspicuous to the officer. He looked at me through the open window, glancing indifferently at my collar, and took my license. He went back to his car, checked the computer database in the event some misdemeanor of mine showed up on it. When he returned, I expected that he would forgive a clergyman on the Lord's business. He gave back my license, placed a ticket in my sweaty hand, and turned two steps to leave. He stopped, retraced his steps, and this was what he said. He said, as though to console me, 'This doesn't mean you are a bad person. It only means you broke the law.'"

"True story, Chen. Honest."

To the policeman's ringing word of endorsement, Chen added her own, "You know, Paul, you really are good person."

I planned to arrive early, thirty minutes before court time. I didn't want to complicate her appearance by a late arrival. It was an old but grand Victorian-style city hall, which housed the courtroom. We entered from the rear entrance off the parking lot. The waiting room was spacious with rows of benches in the center. There was an office window on the left where two or three arrived to pay a fine, buy a license, do something official. Chen reached for her checkbook, preparing for the worst. On the right was the courtroom door. We sat down on the front row of benches facing a long aisle leading to the front entrance. Chen stood up, walked nervously around the room, and sat again, like a mouse cornered by a cat.

"Why so nervous? You weren't so anxious the first time in court, were you? Or were you?"

"That was different. That was U-turn. This was accident, and I was driving too fast—I mean, I was driving in heavy traffic. They will say I was careless."

She got up, walked down the long aisle before us, took a sip from the water fountain at the front entrance, came back, sat down again. "You know, Chen, they're not going to throw you into a dungeon," I said, not a very encouraging way to put it. "I know, I know, but still . . ." The courtroom door opened, and someone led us in. Chen stood shyly off to the left of the official, as though to avoid a direct hit from the court's rebuke. The female magistrate was seated behind a desk, well dressed in civilian clothes. She greeted us with a friendly smile.

"Miss, the trooper who ticketed you has not appeared to confirm the charges. Your case is dismissed. You are free to go."

She was off on a technicality!

Nevertheless, Chen felt unabsolved and began her defense, "But you see, it wasn't my fault. I was driving on left and someone cut me off."

The magistrate's smile broadened. "Miss, listen to me. There are no charges. You're free to go."

I was worried that Chen would charge the absent trooper with making a false arrest. I grabbed my Swan by her right wing, whisked her out of the building back to the car.

"Well well well. What do you know. It seems things turned out all right after all. No trooper, no charges. A fair system, don't you think, Chen?"

"Perhaps . . . Maybe so . . . I guess."

The next day I opened an e-mail: "Dear Paul, I want to thank you for all your help yesterday. And court was good to me."

I took that as an admission that the American justice system was fair and impartial.

The final score: Chen, 1; USA, 1.

Name-Calling

The short stories in our lessons were usually grouped around a given theme. Three stories of unit II handled the theme of prejudice. The lesson for this evening, lesson 6, related a story about a schoolboy named Harry and his sixteen-year-old sister, Silvia. Both names appeared in the first two paragraphs. As always, the three took turns reading the story out loud to practice their English pronunciation. It was Miles's turn to begin. He noticed how some eighteen- or nineteen-year-olds in the story called Harry "Ike."

"Why Ike?" Miles asked. "His name was Harry."

"It's a nickname," I explained. "You have nicknames for each other, don't you? Isn't Miles a nickname?" "No," Chen and Shino said. "We all think that's his real name."

"If maybe you don't know what a nickname is, then let me tell you. It's like another name for a person. It's used to describe someone. We had a player on our baseball team we called Toad. Do you know what a toad is?"

Dr. Who-Knows-Everything claimed he knew, "I've heard the saying that someone at work *toed the line*. It's one of those idioms. I think I know what it means."

"Nope," I said. "That's another word. That's a verb. This was 'toad,' a noun." T-O-A-D, I spelled it out. "It's an animal, like a frog. It's short and squat. My teammate was almost as round in the middle as he was tall. That's why we called him Toad. He had a shape like one."

"That's not very nice," objected Shino. "Wasn't he upset you called him that?"

"We all did," I said. "He didn't mind."

"What did they call you?" Shino asked.

"You know what? My initials are the same for the chemical symbol for—for what? You're a scientist. You must know."

"For lead," Shino answered. "That's right. And it rhymes with head. Get it? You can imagine what they called me."

"I get it," said Shino. "But I would never call you lead head."

"Well, no. I hope not. Not now. But back then you would have. That's what we did then."

"For instance, we had another player whose last name was Herring. Guess what we called him. It was fish." "That's not as bad," said Shino.

I was reluctant to disclose the nickname of another player who had slanted eyes. I did nevertheless. "We called him Chink."

"That's not nice word for Chinese. You mean you would call Miles and Chen chinks?"

"That's OK," the Swan said. "That's what Americans say. We're used to it." Then, smiling all the while, she added, "You should know what we call them." I didn't bother to ask.

Chen looked at Shino. "By way, what do you think they call you?"

I answered for him, "I do remember that when I was a little boy during the war, President Roosevelt—or maybe it was my father, I can't remember—said that we should never refer to them as Japs. We should respectfully call them by their right name—Japanese. He really did say that."

"What did Germans call you?" asked Miles. "When I toured Germany, I visited with a group of them. When someone called me an Ami, I thought it was a compliment. I knew it wasn't when the others said, 'Don't call him that. He's a nice guy.' I saw painted on public buildings over there, years later, 'Amies, go home.' I took it as a hint that we weren't precisely the darlings in Germany we thought we were even then."

"Why is it, do the three of you think, we call people names like these?" I asked, avoiding what other nicknames Chen might have in mind for Americans.

Shino mentioned he read that some universities and baseball teams in America have nicknames. "They are Indian names, like one for Atlantic baseball team. They call them Braves. Some think nicknames like these make certain groups angry. Maybe we shouldn't use them. Although Fish is all right."

I was always impressed by Shino's sensitivity. Did he *ever* bad-mouth people, do the name-calling thing, ridicule them behind their backs? I wondered.

I really didn't know why I got this lesson off on this name-calling tangent.

Miles got us back on track. "I still don't know why they called him Ike." "Let's read on," I said, "and you'll see why."

Shino was reading and came to the sentence where a policeman said to Harry's father, "Don't worry, Mr. Silverstein, we'll take care of you." "That's Jewish name," Shino said. "Harry is Jew."

"Correct," I said, "and 'kike' is a terrible slur on the Jews. They were called kikes, and 'Ike' is a play on that word, don't you see? 'Ike' the 'kike.'"

On the next page, Chen was reading where two guys came out of a pool hall and said something to Sylvia. Chen read, "But she just holds herself tight and goes right on past them both."

"What do you think they said to her?" I asked. "Often the author doesn't relate why a character says something or acts in a certain way. You have to read between the lines and interpret what is meant. What do you think they said?"

"It was something sexual," Chen said. "When she 'holds herself tight,' that means she ignores them. That's what men are like. They're always interested in sex."

"How do you know? Maybe they meant something else," Miles objected.

"Please, Miles," Chen said, "what else would it be? You don't have to defend men."

"You mean you women aren't interested in sex?"

"Not way men are," Chen answered.

This was one of those occasional snippy exchanges between Chen and Miles. Miles could sometimes get under a person's skin. He did it several times with Chen.

A Christian Nation?

The lesson 6 story described how a group of boys beat up on Harry. They overthrew the stand of newspapers Harry was selling for his father on a New York City street. Harry fell on one of the *New York Times* editions, which reported how people were fleeing from Hitler's approaching army. Silvia screamed at the watching crowd to help. "What's the use? All those people standing around and none of them would help." And then, "They pick on us Jews because we're weak and haven't got any country."

I asked them to notice the title of the story: "Prelude." "Do you know what the word 'prelude' means?" They didn't, so I explained, "It's something—a piece of music, a short talk, or, like here, a story—that comes before the main part. Now look at the footnote. When does it say the story was written?" "In 1938," Shino said. "That's before start of World War II."

"You see," I said, "the story is prophetic. The author could not have known at the time, could he, the terrible persecution the Jews suffered under Hitler? The story is a prelude. What happened after Harry and Sylvia, with those guys picking on them, was far worse. Millions of Jews died."

When I taught college students back in the '80s and '90s, we chastised ourselves for how little—if any—history of China and Japan was in our curriculum. But now, it appeared, how little my three learned about European history. They usually drew a blank when I mentioned Henry VIII or the French Revolution or the Crusades or the Reformation era. Shino, however, had traveled widely in Europe and had read up on World War II on the continent. He already knew enough about Japan's involvement in the

Pacific theater. Miles watched the History Channel while in the USA. He saw for himself the horrendous results of the Holocaust in Hitler's Germany.

This provided my Bumblebee with one of his stinging barbs. He said, "How could such horrible thing happen in *Christian* nation?"—with the emphasis on 'Christian.' Shino drew on his pool of historical information and began to describe the conditions—economic, political—which led to the rise of Hitler.

Miles kept pressing the issue. "This was *Christian* nation. How could *Christians* do that to Jews?"

I made some small attempt to tell the other side of the story. "There were Christians," I told them, "who befriended the Jews. Gertraud's parents, for instance, kept some Jewish friends in their house for two days till they got them out of Germany to New York." I asked them if they ever heard of Dietrich Bonhoeffer. "He was a brilliant theologian," I explained, "who abandoned a promising career to speak out against the Nazis. He was finally hanged for participating with other officers in a plot to take Hitler's life. We have his inspiring letters from prison, smuggled out by friendly guards."

I had brought Bonhoeffer's book *Letters and Papers from Prison* and showed it to them. Chen leaned forward and reached for it. "May I borrow it? I'd like to read it."

I looked at Miles. I wanted to get at what we mean by "Christian." "Just because a person tries to live a good life, like you do, doesn't make you a Christian, does it?" "I'm not a Christian," he replied.

"I know, I know. But just because you live in the USA, what people call a Christian nation, doesn't make you a Christian either, right?" "Of course not." "And if someone stamped Made in China on a package with a radio made by Mexicans, that doesn't make the radio Chinese, does it?" "Not if it was made by Mexicans," he said. "What I'm getting at, it's what is on the inside that makes a person a Christian. Just because you stamp Christian on Germany doesn't mean that each and every German was a Christian." "Hitler certainly was not Christian," Shino added.

You will remember I mentioned that when I began teaching ESL, I would not use the course to argue them into Christianity. I did want to share the Gospel with them, and it was always in the back of my mind, but I would do it in an offhand manner if the occasion presented itself in a natural way. I concluded this was such an occasion. So I said to Miles, "Now, what if when you return to China—certainly not what we would call a Christian nation—something happened to you while here on your inside. Say you came to believe that there is a god after all, that this god revealed himself in human form, that he died on the cross for what wrong you do, that you then knew that god is your friend—and not because of all the good you do—and that he loves you as if you were the only person in the world. What if you came to believe that? That would make you a Christian even in China, wouldn't it?"

Miles rushed his hand over his jet-black hair. He shook his head. "No. Jesus was good man. I suppose he was anyway. That's what I think. I don't know about all this other stuff."

I was attempting to throw out some Gospel seed, hoping it would fall on fertile ground. So far, it appeared, it landed on rocky soil.

The exercises that followed this story contained sentences based on a 1938 edition of the *New York Times*. Each sentence contained five underlined words, one of which was deliberately misspelled. They were to identify the mistake and write the correction on the accompanying blank.

Sentence 9 read, "Churches will hold special services *tomorrow* to *celebrate* Ash *Wendesday* and there will be special services daily in many of the churches *throughout* the *forty* days of Lent." They all caught the misspelling and wrote "Wednesday" on the blank.

Chen was puzzled by what the sentence was describing. I explained what Lent was and mentioned that Immanuel conducts services each Wednesday during the period. "I'm involved in some of the services," I said.

"I'd like to see you work some time," Miles said. Chen and Shino were more specific. "Could we come to hear you speak? Would that be OK?"

"Sure, of course," I said. "I'll let you know when I'm scheduled."

I wondered if they were serious. At any rate, I wasn't going to hold my breath till one of them appeared.

A Visit to Van Andel

I wasn't going to hold my breath till any one of them appeared for a worship service and "see me work" as Miles put it. I wasn't sure, anyway, if they were ready to comprehend a full-length homily. And I knew the way we worshiped would only confuse them. But I asked them later if I could come to Van Andel and *see them work*.

"I'd like to get inside the institute and take a look at where you do your research. Would any of you be able to take me on a tour of Van Andel? Anyone?" I asked.

"Sure, of course," they all said as with one voice. "We'd be happy to."

"But you're all so busy. I don't want to interrupt your experiments." "We're not *that* busy for *you*," said Chen cheerfully. Miles said he was conducting an important experiment these days. He might not be able to leave it for a long tour. He could, however, pause to show me his work at his office. Shino said he would join Chen on the tour. We arranged a time of a day for next week.

I had always eyed Van Andel's western edge from the church's side. It looked to me that the building, perched like an eagle on a hill, glared down from far above. It dwarfed the church and parking lot, which separated the two buildings. Van Andel's four-story glass-enclosed offices and meeting rooms overawed many of us looking up from below. It surely did me.

I parked my Buick Skylark in the church's lot, walked up Michigan Street one block, around the corner another half block to the east-side entrance. A wide semicircle driveway faced the entrance with its glass doorways. A half-dozen or so gigantic planters—filled with some sort of foliage—were set a few yards before the entrance. Their intent was to prevent some terrorist, I suppose, or some vandals from ramming their vehicles through the doors. No one simply walked through those doors. They were all locked to the general public. It was a forbidding sight. Would they allow me in?

Of course, they would. I knew because Chen would have arranged things. I guess I'm easily intimidated.

I noticed a doorbell and a speaker, however, on the sidewall. When I rang it and announced that I was an invited guest, I heard a click, which unlocked the door. I entered.

I proceeded across an expansive, empty foyer. A long, broad stairway led to the second floor. One young lady sat on a cushioned chair behind a lengthy reception desk. Over the area hung a colorful decorative design from a high ceiling. I later learned from another Chinese scientist that it was an image of DNA, constructed at the cost of $300,000. The lobby all looked so elegant and first class that I felt out of place, as though it were meant only for distinguished public figures.

When I mentioned Chen and Shino, "Of course," the young lady said, "they are expecting you," and rang their office phones. I registered my name and the time when I arrived as required. She attached a name badge to my coat lapel.

I experienced the same procedure a year later when Chen led me and Gertraud's cousin, visiting here from Germany, on a tour. The receptionist then was new. She didn't recognize Chen's name, or at least how I pronounced it. However, when I mentioned Miles's name, "Yes, of course," she said, "everybody knows Miles."

"Hi, Paul," I heard Chen's cheerful, welcoming voice as she was descending the stairway along with Shino. They both had their identification badges hanging from their sides. "We're glad you came. We'll take you on tour."

They gave me such a royal welcome I felt like a state official visiting from a foreign government. Shino stood on my right, like a member of an honor guard. Chen linked her arm under my left elbow and guided me toward the stairway. I enjoyed how celebrated they made me feel, like the arrival of an Olympic gold medalist.

They led me up the long stairway and then down a corridor with open rooms on the right and left. The Chinese and Japanese scientists, whom I recognized as members of our other ESL classes, looked up from their desks and gave me a glad hello. Chen proudly introduced me to her American colleagues with "Paul is my ESL teacher," as though I was a Harvard graduate school professor.

Chen took me into a lab. She showed me a glass container where something was swimming around. "Here's where we grow cancer cells." Most of us preparing to be ministers were naturally more interested in the social sciences—like psychology—than the physical sciences. That helps to explain why I was an absolute flop at biology in college. That's also why I asked some silly questions, some born out of pure ignorance, some simply to get a rise out of Chen.

"Why are you growing cancer cells? I thought you were supposed to cure cancer, not create it." I was egging her on, but she wasn't a bit fazed.

"We inject cancer cells into mice to see how they grow and how we can control them."

"But we're not mice," I objected. "Close enough," said Chen.

Shino took me into labs and offices, which only he had the authority to enter. Chen had to remain outside. He used his personally assigned card to enter a lab where a single scientist was at work. Since Shino was tight-lipped about the experiment, I gathered the research was highly secretive and asked no questions. So on to other rooms and labs not apparently accessible to other scientists. I said, "My word, Shino, you must be an important person around here." A subdued, slight smile creased the corners of his mouth. "Not really, Paul." That was Shino again, as unpretentious as always.

We finally came to Miles's office where he sat over his experiment. He had dissected several mice. He showed me their inner organs. For me it was a slimy sight.

When I was a young parish pastor, I nearly fainted when seeing the open wound of a hospitalized member. Blood made a hasty retreat from my head when standing bedside. I feared I would pass out. Others noticed my pale face and joked, "Pastor, maybe you should get in the next bed." I compensated then by "accidentally" dropping something on the floor. Bending down, I fumbled around for the "lost" item till the blood backtracked and I was able to stand upright. Even now, gory scenes on television or in the movies force me to turn my head.

As far as I was concerned, Miles did not need to identify each and every slimy exposed organ of his "sacrificed" mice and dangle it before my face. But he was in his element, and I kept watching. I screwed up my courage, as silly as it might seem, as I observed the dismembered and sliced-up mice. I tell you, I could never be a surgeon, or a scientist for that matter, cutting mice apart.

The three informed me that they were not always trying to discover the cure for cancer. "It's so hard to find cure," they all said. "There are so many different kinds." Instead, they searched for ways to prevent its spread. That's what Miles was researching.

Why was it, he was investigating, that a cancer cell, say in the colon, could spread somewhere else, to the liver perhaps? He spelled out his work in such complicated technical terms, however, that it passed right over my head. I asked him to explain in laymen's terms.

"You live here in Grand Rapids," he began. "Let's imagine you want to buy cottage near Grand Haven." It was some forty miles away.

"You look at one. You can't buy it because it costs too much. You see another, but it's too small. You search for cottage till you find one that's just right. So then you settle in. Cancer cells are like that. They conduct search throughout body, way you looked for cottage, until—"

"Until they can find a place they can afford," I interrupted.

"Correct. Well, something like that. They send out spies for land it's easy to invade. I search these days why certain cells find inviting beachhead somewhere and can wade right in."

When pressed to explain, Miles's answers were always like that—illustrated and down to earth. He was so good at it I regarded him a born teacher. I told him so. "You should apply to get a teaching position at one of our universities. You have the degrees, and many schools favor diversity on their faculties. Why not do it?"

"I'm just interested in research," he answered.

As we concluded the tour, I impressed upon them how critical their research was. "I've had so many friends who died of cancer," I said. I related this story about one of them.

"Heiner Sell was a famous doctor in Manhattan. He and his wife were Germans, whom we met at our church. Naturally, Gertraud and I became friends with them. One Memorial Day, our families joined together on the Bronxville school grounds for a picnic, which the residents arranged. Both Heiner and I were beginning to feel ill. After a while, 'I'm getting sick, in pain,' Heiner said. 'Would you drive me home?' I did and then went home since I was feeling under the weather myself.

"I only had an upset stomach, but Heiner's problem was deadly. Seven months later, in unbearable pain, Heiner was rushed from his Catskill summer home to the hospital where he practiced. After his colleagues operated on him, they returned to his recovery room with tears in their eyes.

"He had inoperable cancer! He had three to four months to live!

"The next months I called on Heiner in his home. I prayed with him and read selected psalms for his comfort. 'Do you know what psalms are?' I asked them. 'They are like prayers from the Bible.' Anyway, he was continually in severe pain, but never complained. Nor did he lose his faith in Jesus throughout his ordeal. To this day, I remember him as a saintly child of God.

"I visited him in the hospital," I continued the story, "where he spent his last weeks. Disregarding the No Visitors Allowed sign on his door, I entered anyway because he eagerly welcomed me for prayer and scripture readings. 'You know, Paul,' he once told me, 'I could end all this suffering by jumping out that window.' We were perhaps on the ninth floor. 'But you're not going to do that, Heiner, are you?' 'No, Paul, of course not.'

"Easter Sunday morning, we held a brief worship with his wife and three young children around his bed. With quiet composure, he prepared his family for his impending death. He died soon thereafter. The church was packed with friends, colleagues, and former patients, where we celebrated the life of a devout Christian physician. The cemetery grounds near his Catskill home received his cremated remains."

I told this whole story in detail to my three friends. I deliberately emphasized Heiner's faith in Christ. I stressed his unfailing trust that with death, God would hold him in his loving arms. They listened attentively, solemnly. "There are more stories like that about my friends," I added. "But not now. I need to be on my way," I announced, thanking them for the tour. "Besides, you have work to do on this dreadful disease."

I intended Heiner's story to serve as another little Gospel seed scattered at their feet—an attempt to indirectly "share the Gospel" in story form. Would it take root in any one of them, or was their soil still unprepared to receive? I wondered about it all the way home.

This visit was time well spent. I'm glad I showed interest in their work as they had in mine. Such reciprocity furthered the endless process of transcending our cultural differences—even with occasional setbacks. It can happen, I came to realize, only if we were willing to get inside each other—like an MRI—to examine how and why we were put together. Of course, this takes time. And a bona fide commitment to put ourselves in one another's shoes.

As the months passed, I concluded that I was a father figure for Chen. She often spoke about her father and certainly missed him. I connected with Chen because I was his stand-in for her, I'm sure, her link with her father back home. With Shino, it was mostly religion that connected us with each other, more so than with Chen at first and surely more than with Miles.

As for Miles, I wasn't clear what kind of a figure I was for him. As an Asian, I knew he respected old age. Religion obviously came between us, but never at the cost of mutual care and concern. We were friends—not perhaps like the Old Testament bosom buddies David and Jonathan, but friends nevertheless—and good ones. If you would ask me now to pick a favorite among the three—well, I couldn't do it. It would be like trying, blindfolded, to untie a tangled knot with no hands.

Still, the way Chen, Shino, and Miles embraced my presence that day at Van Andel replaced the tie I had with those college students with whom I also became close friends. These three contradicted my self-image of a newcomer to Grand Rapids, playing second fiddle in these parts, with a sore back, a gimpy knee, and a memory that failed me from time to time. What a contrast to these fast-stepping, nimble, energetic young bodies and brains! They lifted my spirits week after week.

"Rided," "Shooted," and
Ludicrous Mistakes

They joined ESL to expand their vocabulary. That was uppermost in their minds. But I soon decided to point out their mistakes in English grammar and usages.

You can imagine how difficult it was for them to understand the irregularities in the English language. These all meant sense to me. I grew up with them. They all came naturally to me without wondering why it was *ei* in "receive" but not in "believe." I took it for granted they'd recognize the need to correct their mistakes.

Chen didn't always take the need for granted. "I rided with Shino to the airport," she e-mailed me. She meant to write, "I drove Shino to the airport," for that is what she did; he was off to attend a conference out of state. Should I choose to correct her "rided" with "drove" or indicate that there is no such word as "rided"? I chose the former. "The past tense of 'ride' is 'rode,'" I said, "not 'rided.' You should have e-mailed that you rode with Shino."

"Why not 'rided'?" she asked. "Why can't I just add *d* to the end of 'ride'? That makes it simple. I do that with other words. What's wrong with that?"

"Like what other words?" I asked.

"Like 'live.' Past of 'live' is 'lived.' That's why I just put *d* at end of 'ride.' I don't make 'live' into 'lode.' You wouldn't say you used to lode in New York, but now you live in Grand Rapids."

Chen was getting more and more sure of herself as she went on.

"I do same with 'decide.' I decided to come to America. I just put *d* at end. See how I do it? I've never heard anyone say he decode to do something."

It was hard to quarrel with her sense of logic.

Miles had the same trouble. I asked him about his experiments on human cancer tumors.

"Where do you get the cancer tissue?" I asked.

"From morgue. From dead bodies in morgue," he answered, matter-of-factly.

"From the morgue? How could you use bodies from the morgue?"

"They were criminals. No one claimed their bodies. They got shooted by police."

"You mean 'shot.' It is incorrect to say shooted. Drop one *o* and the *ed*. Better to say 'they got shot by the police.'"

Miles objected to my correction. He raised his eyebrows as he prepared a rebuttal. He described how he rooted for the Chinese in the Olympics. "I didn't rot for them," he said. "Besides, when I start my computer, I boot it up. Then when I talk in past, I say 'booted.' I keep extras *o* and *ed*."

Although he was correct, of course, about "booted," I was at a loss to explain why it's not "shooted."

Shino had less difficulties with English. Except for one little word. There is no definite article in Japanese or in Chinese. (You have already noticed that.) It was not uncommon for him, as well as for the others, to say, "I will open door for you," or, "Yes, I will come to pizza party." That "the" was an unnecessary pesky insect they swatted when it got in their way.

Here it was easier for them to see that we employ the definite article. They occasionally remembered to stick "the" where it belonged or even "a," although they must have wondered why.

However, it puzzled them why it was incorrect to use "he" or "she *say* something or another." "It was perfectly correct," I explained, "to combine 'I' or 'we' or 'you' or 'they' with 'say.' But when it's 'he' or 'she,' you should add *s*. He or 'she *says* this or that.' You need to do that with other verbs too, like 'think' or 'guess.'" "But why?" Miles asked. "Why add *s* with those two but not other four? Why not 'I say*s*'?"

I summarized perfectly, I thought, the reasons for these needed repairs in their English usages by quoting Gertraud: "The English language makes no sense."

Chen usually said, "I *think* so," to answer my several queries. The verb was always emphasized, as though she placed a question mark behind her "think," as though to say "I hope so." She sounded uncertain the way she dragged out "thiinnk."

After one of our get-togethers, I asked her, "Did you enjoy our party? Did you like the pizza?" She said, "I *think* so." That sounded to me more like, "I guess so."

"You mean you didn't have a good time?" I asked.

"Of course, I did. I loved everything—party, pizza, also scotch."

"You had scotch? I didn't notice that."

"I took some sips from Shino's glass. No one was looking." Why she thought she had to drink scotch secretly remains a mystery to me.

"You like scotch?" Again her "I *think* so" seemed merely to infer a possible likelihood for the taste. Did she mean, "I'm not sure. Maybe?" But at a later party she revealed her true feelings. She really meant, "I certainly did!"

"At times, use a stronger verb than 'think' to express your opinions," I said. "You wouldn't answer that you think cancer is awful if I asked you, would you? You'd be more emphatic than that. Get what I mean?"

She got what I meant. "Sorry, Paul. I didn't mean to say I didn't like party . . . At least, I *think* so," she said as she deliberately emphasized the word and then laughed. So did I.

"Listen, Chen, you'd be surprised—or maybe you wouldn't—how often I've used a poor choice of words. I don't know if I ever told you how, when in college, I asked my prof, 'How *low* do you go?'"

"What you mean by that?" Miles asked, astonished. "Doesn't that make people think they drop down to something bad?"

Shino added, "In Japan, students don't say that to their teachers. At least, they would not say like that to me."

"Well, I didn't just step up to my prof and say that to his face. We were having a bull session during class. Do you know what a bull session' is?" (We were about to launch into another idiom.)

"I've heard the saying shooting the bull. Or is it 'shotting' the bull?" Miles was getting back at me, teasing me. "Is that what you did?"

"No, you're correct, it's 'shooting.' And an actual bull is not meant. It means to engage in idle talk. It's like when we say 'shooting the breeze.'"

I came back to my college Greek prof. "I confess, sometimes I didn't prepare the translations. Some others didn't either. So we tried to distract him with questions to avoid the assignment. We attempted a bull session."

"How did you do that?" Shino asked. "I don't know if my students ever tried that with me. Must be American way."

"It was easy. At times he even invited it. He was also a music critic and wrote reviews for the local newspaper. In one, he criticized the bowing of a solo violinist. 'He didn't move his fiddle correctly over the strings,' he told us, 'didn't *bow* it properly. But then a woman criticized me in a letter. "The violinist's *bowing* was just fine," she wrote me. "He leaned over just far enough to recognize the applause."

"He had to laugh about it."

"That was his hint that he welcomed questions about his side job as a music critic. We jumped in with questions to fill up the entire hour. One after the other of us came up with them to keep the bull session going. He went along with it. He was flattered by our feigned interest in his role as a music critic.

"He also reviewed recordings of the masters: Bach, Beethoven, Brahms. Someone asked him about them. I knew he didn't stoop to review Frank Sinatra and Perry Como. But I wondered about notables like George Gershwin. I didn't quite know how to put it. I blurted out, 'How low do you go?' It was a real blunder. He was offended. The class scolded me, 'You don't talk like that to our prof.' They weren't serious. They were phonies trying to score points with him. The look he gave me made me feel I had flunked the course right then and there."

"So your own language gets you into trouble," Chen was glad to notice.

"Not only English," I said. "German too."

"You speak German?" Shino asked.

"Well, somewhat. I had a great German teacher in high school. She had us memorize twenty vocables each week. I did pretty well with them. But many years later, when I toured Europe with my friend Mike, I messed up badly with my choice of words in German."

I told the three how. "Mike was a German living in America. He planned to visit his aged mother in Berlin, and I went along. Our final day there, she prepared a delicious meal for us. It was a tender moment because Mike realized he might never see her again. When we were ready to leave, she asked me, in German of course, if I had enough to eat. I was in hot water when I answered, 'Ich habe satt,' which means in English 'I'm fed up.' Her face fell. She was deeply hurt. Why? I wondered. What did I say wrong? 'No, no,' Mike rescued me. 'Paul means "Ich bin satt," which means 'I'm well satisfied.'

"I well nigh ruined those final sentimental minutes between Mike and his mother. With tears in his eyes, he gave her a long emotional hug. Then silently he led me out the door before I could say another word."

"Weren't you embarrassed?" Chen asked. "Of course, I was. I resolved thereafter to connect the correct verbs with the German *satt*."

"But the Germans weren't much better when they attempted English," I went on. "That showed up when Gertraud and I were married in her hometown. The evening before we were married, we visited her pastor. We wanted him to sanction our marriage. It was a formality because we knew he would. We met anyway. He asked about how we met, our common interests, and so on, the usual matters that occupied these interviews. At the conclusion, for my sake, he reassured us in English, 'I support this marriage with my whole soul and *bottom*.'"

"He meant 'body,'" Miles laughed. "We knew he did but managed not to laugh and kept a strait face. We didn't correct his English. We didn't dare."

After this lengthy bull session of our own, we began the evening's lesson. All my efforts to correct their English ran into a snag when we read the story "The Good Lord Will Provide." I failed to inform them what the teacher's manual indicated. "The material in this story is not Standard English," the manual noted. "The lesson treats dialects, the way some people talk informally in a given setting." The story contained letters written by Walt, a "dumb" farmer as he described himself to his wife Judy.

As usual, the group took turns reading out loud. Miles came to the opening sentence of the fifth paragraph. "When Ike heard the news on the radio, he knowed right off—," and then Miles stopped. He felt vindicated! "See, Paul, that's what I mean. The verb is 'know,' and when he makes it past tense, he sort of does what I do. He simply adds *ed*. But he should have added another *o*."

"Yes," added Chen, "same for me. I just read, 'Judy, it's not like I done anything wrong.' He should have written 'did anything wrong.' If Walt is wrong when he says 'done,' or even 'dided,' why did you say I should have e-mailed 'rode' instead of 'rided'?"

"Wait a minute. Let me explain. The lesson demonstrates how some people do not use Standard English. It's called dialect. Remember, Walt called himself a 'dumb' farmer. Of course, he would have written 'stupid' in Standard English. But that's how some people talk among themselves. I once admitted to Gertraud that I did a dumb thing. I wouldn't use 'dumb' when I preach, for instance, when I mean 'stupid.'"

"Did Gertraud agree that you did dumb thing?" Chen giggled.

"Probably," I said. "But that's not the point. I'm simply trying to show how we sometimes speak in private among friends."

Then I told Miles, "Walt should have written in Standard English 'he should have known' instead of 'he knowed.' Chen, you're also right. He should have written 'it's not like I did anything wrong,' but never 'dided.'"

"Or," Shino added, "Walt could have written 'he should have known' instead of 'he knowed.' He could have written in correct English 'it's not like I had done anything wrong' instead of 'I done anything wrong.'"

Shino's pool of perfect grammar impressed me.

"I should have told you to begin with that this is not Standard English. It's about dialect. Sorry I confused you."

"That's OK," Miles said. "Our language has dialects too. Many of them. The way we use nonstandard Chinese would confuse you."

"I'm already confused. You spell your last name *xie*, with a small *x*," I told Chen. "You even list your last name first. How come? We do the very opposite. I'm always Paul Boecler."

"That's just way it is," said Chen. "Besides, maybe we do it better."

"Do your languages ever confuse words that sound almost the same but with different meanings?" I asked, changing the subject.

"You mean like word 'bow' in your violinist's story?" Shino recalled.

"No, that's spelled the same. I mean words like 'vowels' and 'bowels,' words that almost sound the same though spelled differently. I had a colleague in New York who taught an ESL course," I told them. "She had a terrible headache the day a foreign student told her, 'I'm having trouble with my bowels.'"

"Bowels?" she asked, amazed.

"Yes, bowels."

"I can't help you with your bowels. You need to see a doctor for that."

"But you're the expert. Can't you help me? I get two of them in the wrong order."

"You can't get your bowels in the wrong order. You were created like that."

"You mean there's no rule I can learn to get them in the right order?"

"What in heaven's name are you talking about?" she said, her head throbbing with each exchange. "Of course, there's no such rule."

"There must be. Why is it *ei* in 'receive' but not in 'believe'? I always get marked down when I write 'recieve.'"

"Ah, 'vowels' you mean. Like *a, e, i, o, u*. You mean 'vowels,' not 'bowels.'"

"You mean they're not the same?"

My colleague swallowed another aspirin.

Haggling

I often wondered how Miles and Chen felt as foreigners—and Chinese at that—when here on our soil. Must they not have sensed that Americans regard the Chinese differently than say, the Japanese and Germans? You know, how people say, "You can't trust the Chinese." Then there was that hostile American who told Chen, "You Chinese steal our technology." And, "You're unfair when you trade with us." Would my Chinese put their best foot forward to rebut such charges like the accused defending themselves in court?

Well, let's see.

The days of the ugly American still lingered in Germany when I spent a year at the University of Tuebingen. "See, another pushy American"—I didn't want to be painted with that brush. Therefore, I didn't quibble over the price of a broken-down Simca automobile. I should have. It wasn't worth a nickel when I left Germany a year later.

I can't speak for Miles. But Chen and I were hardly carbon copies of each other. Complaints of Chinese swindling and duplicity and getting the upper hand didn't faze her one bit. That was apparent—right in step with American culture, by the way—when she haggled over the price of new tires for her Toyota. Or over its replacement when she totaled it on the interstate. I already told you about that. Remember, it wasn't her fault. At least, that's how the story went.

"Paul, I need to buy new tires. Do you know where I can get best buy?" she asked after class.

"I just bought some for our Passat. I got a great deal from a discount dealer."

"What's address?"

"You'll have a hard time finding it." Then I offered, "Want me to take you there?"

"Yeah, sure. I'd like that. Thanks."

I met her at Van Andel. She drove. I hung on to my seat as she wove in and out of traffic on the interstate, cutting off some cars in the process. I asked her, "Where did you learn to drive—in China?"

"No, no. We had no car. I rided bicycle." (See. She still insisted it's not "rode.")

"Then you learned here in Grand Rapids?"

"I took two lessons. It was easy to get license."

I think she was exaggerating. "Only two lessons? Didn't they teach you how to drive on the interstate?"

"I didn't need it. Why you ask?"

"Oh, nothing," I said.

When we left the interstate, we turned on to Twenty-eighth Street and drew near the entrance to the dealer. I mistakenly directed her into the wrong lot filled with parked cars. I couldn't have made a worse mistake.

"Sorry," I said, "you need to turn around." "No problem," Chen reassured me. "I can do that." I worried she'd bump into the other vehicles. Then she'd have another problem on her hands, another possible court appearance. It took her two moves to turn around, first lurching into reverse, then propelling forward, then reverse, and forward again. All this in fifteen seconds. I imagine she wanted to impress me with her driving prowess. We exited, narrowly avoiding a collision. I breathed a sigh of relief. So did the parked cars.

The salesman recognized me. "This is Chen. She is my Chinese friend. She needs some new tires." I pointed to the brand of tires I bought. "Look, Chen. They are a good buy."

She pretended to be disinterested and looked away. "What about those tires over there?" she asked. "I see their price is lower."

"They won't last as long," the salesman said. "You're better off with the kind Paul bought. Honest." He was correct, but Chen stalled.

"Hmmm . . . I don't know. What about tires I see in corner. Maybe they don't cost as much."

"They won't hold the road as well in the winter. You know what the Michigan roads are like in the winter. All those potholes. Right, Paul?" I nodded yes.

"Don't you have other tires?" Chen asked.

"Not for the size you need. Unless you drive a semi," he giggled. Chen kept a straight face. Then she frowned at him.

I was embarrassed—though Chen wasn't—by this endless haggling. "Really, Chen, the ones I bought are the better tires—and a better buy."

"I don't have much money. Maybe I should go to other store." This was her ace in the hole that brought the salesman to his knees. Now he felt a sale slipping through his fingers.

"All right, I'll tell you what. I'll give you the same tires Paul bought but at a reduced sales price."

"Well, OK. I guess I can do that," she said, as though she were doing him a favor.

Back in her Toyota, new tires and all, and after examining each and every one of them with a critical eye, I told her, "You'd make a great capitalist."

"Why you say that? We all try to get best deal back home."

I later learned how similar our cultures are—especially for Chen and Gertraud. When purchasing a new car, our women shared the same idiosyncrasy. At least that's what I'd call it. They would call it aesthetic sensitivity.

When we moved to Grand Rapids, we bought a second car. It had to be German made, Gertraud insisted. Fair enough, I thought.

The Passat dealer showed us several models. I searched for the lowest price; Gertraud searched for the right color. "What about this one?" I said. "It's a thousand dollars cheaper." "But it's not the right color," Gertraud complained. Yes, of course, it has to be the right color. What was I thinking?

We wound up buying the more expensive silver Passat. Never mind the price. It had to be the right color.

Chen found from a newspaper ad to replace her wrecked Toyota. Naturally, it had to be foreign made. I drove her to the street address where Frank's used Honda was parked. Chen emerged from her side and approached the Honda as if a detective at a crime scene looking for clues.

She found one.

"Look at that scratch," she exclaimed. It was a long, razor-thin scratch, reaching diagonally across the black hood from one side to the other. To Chen, it stood out like a lightning bolt across the midnight sky. She rubbed it, as though to remove the disaster. It stood still.

"What price you asking?" "Eighty-one hundred," Frank answered. "That's little high. I was hoping for less. How about $7,900?"

"What? I can't go down that much. It's too good a car for that."

I stood off to the side watching the drama unfold.

"What about the battery?" "It's almost brand-new," Frank said. "Really?" Chen questioned. "Yes, really. I recently replaced it. Don't you believe me?" "Sure, sure," she said. "I was just *thinking.*"

Chen kept investigating. About the tires. About the mileage. She examined the upholstery. Sadly, she discovered no incriminating evidence to haggle the price lower.

Still, there was that horrible scratch on the hood she remembered. "Couldn't you take hundred off because of it?" Chen asked.

"You're worried too much about the appearance. Think about its value, its durability, how it rides. You're going to drive it, aren't you, not admire it?" Frank scored an important point, though he clearly did not understand feminine values. No wonder he was divorced, as he had announced earlier.

"That big scratch still bothers me," Chen complained, ignoring Frank's emphasis on the Honda's more significant attributes. As though that mattered most to Chen.

Frank finally relented. He took the hundred off.

Then Chen circled the car. "Look," she said. There were five-foot-long thin scratches on the rear. She giggled as she rubbed each one. Chen suggested they were worth another fifty off the price.

Exasperated, Frank said, "Why don't you search under the car too. Maybe you'll find more scratches there." "I don't have to see them when I drive it," Chen laughed. "Let me think about it. I'll call you tomorrow."

All the way back to Van Andel, Chen kept murmuring about how the hood looked with that long scratch. I tried to minimize her concern by joking, "Just think, for as long as you drive this car, you'll have to see in front of you that dreadful, ugly, obscene gash on the hood."

The next day, I talked to Chen before class.

"Did Frank take that extra $50 off?"

"Yeah, sure. He was good about it."

"So you bought the car?"

"No, I cancelled deal."

I was flabbergasted. "But why?"

"That *awful scratch!* On hood!"

I grabbed my forehead, dumbfounded.

Chen and Gertraud: cultural carbon copies of each other.

Miles versus Chen

Miles and Lin were frequent moviegoers. They often went to the theater. More often they watched videos at home. Dozens of them. One of them was with Clark Gable and Vivien Leigh in *Gone with the Wind*.

"That's such an oldie. Why watch *that*?" I asked.

"We can't in China. Government won't let us. They think it will make us want civil war. They are afraid." He shook his head in utter disbelief. He was as critical of his government's policies as he was of any religion.

Martin Luther was in town those days—the movie, not the Reformer. I was glad Miles proposed we all go to see it—and surprised since I assumed he knew it involved religion.

"How about a Saturday matinee and a pizza party after it? Gertraud and I will meet you at Van Andel. We'll all drive from there," I suggested before our class began.

"It's better you go right from your place. That's shorter for you. You won't waste time," said Miles, our mother hen. "I'll drive us from Van Andel and meet you there. I can find best time for movie."

They had arrived before we did, and Shino, Chen, and Lin waited for us in the parking lot. Miles, already at the theater's entrance, directed us to the box office. He was in charge, like a traffic cop, and assigned the aisle where we were to sit. Chen and Gertraud sat next to each other with Lin. Shino and Miles sat to my right.

I wondered how they would react to Luther's discovery of the Gospel and his "here I stand" before church and state. "This will be interesting," I told Gertraud. As we filed out the theater, Miles was more than pleased that Luther opposed the state. Predictably, he ignored the religious element. He told Shino and me, "Diversity is always good thing in society."

Shino glanced back at me and whispered, "He didn't get it, did he?" Clearly, Miles "didn't get" Luther's spiritual struggle. That didn't surprise me. Though I wondered about the "it" Shino said Miles "didn't get." What did Shino mean by the "it"? Luther's search for God's grace? Is that what Shino meant? Was this a sign that he was not far from the Kingdom? Was he a closet Christian after all?

Gertraud was preparing the pizzas in the kitchen, just adjacent to the TV room where the rest of us were gathered. Miles sat next to me on a ledge in front of the fireplace. Shino, Lin, and Chen sat on the couch facing us.

"How about some scotch, Chen? You're not driving. Want to try it? Shino and I are having some." "Sure," she said, standing up. "I'll try it." I didn't want to give away our little secret that she had previously sipped some scotch from Shino's glass "when no one was looking."

I filled her glass. She took a sip. "Ummm, tastes good," she said innocently, like an explorer who had just discovered virgin territory. She took another sip, set her glass down, and took her seat.

Miles, inspired by Luther's defiance of Charles V, began to criticize China's government. "It's wrong that they allow only one child for parents." This was the rebel speaking. The patriot took up a defense. "That's not so," Chen answered. "Couples can have more than one child in rural areas. Besides, we must limit population."

She took her third sip of scotch, a fuller one this time.

They squared off against one another, something like Richard Nixon's kitchen debate with Nikita Khrushchev.

Here is a short excerpt from some of their exchanges.

The Rebel: There is denial of human rights, no freedom of speech.
The Patriot: There is need for stability and control. There has been much upset in our history.
The Rebel: Government officials are corrupt and unjust.
The Patriot: We have many independent judges and prosecutors.

Chen's glass was nearly empty. I topped it off with more scotch. She took another sip.

"Here comes your pizza, Miles." Gertraud had remembered that Miles was allergic to cheese and had prepared a cheeseless one for him. Then, "Whoops!" exclaimed Gertraud. The pizza slipped off the pan, and gravity took over. Miles leaped from his seat and flew into the kitchen. I swear, he knew what was happening almost before it did. The Bumblebee arrived at the accident scene seconds after the pizza fell dead, facedown on the floor. "Don't touch it," he insisted. "I can fix it." He grabbed a spatula and slid it deftly, like a scalpel, under the deceased remains and resurrected it faceup on a plate. "There. No harm done. Let's eat," he said.

We all applauded. Another successful emergency room operation by Dr. Miles.

However, we saved the soiled pizza for Miles.

Chen was feeling her oats between bites from her pizza and sips from her scotch. In fairly fluent English, she was getting the upper hand in crossing swords with Miles over Chinese politics.

Here I must pause to illustrate why Chen's English improved immeasurably as the debate wore on.

I spent my year of vicarage—it's like an internship—in New York City before I graduated from the seminary. It was the busiest year of my life. I regularly taught evening classes, and one time in particular, I was not fully prepared. It was my supervisor's pastor's birthday, and the family invited me to help celebrate with a drink before my class.

"I don't have time," I objected, "I need this time to prepare." "Come over anyway," they urged, "you can spare an hour." I had one Manhattan—or maybe it was two—all on an empty stomach. When I left for class, I felt my tongue and mind miraculously liberated. George Herbert once said, "Where the drink goes in, there the wit goes out." I don't know about wit, but at that class, I was the most knowledgeable and articulate theologian in all New York City.

I cannot do justice by putting into words how articulate Chen became the rest of the evening. Vocables we never learned in ESL came out of the blue.

Her sentences ran as smooth as China silk. Her grammar was as flawless as one had a right to expect. She even included an occasional definite article, plus an indefinite one.

Miles was losing ground in the debate with Chen over China's repressive tactics. (Of course, Chen had an advantage. She drank scotch; Miles had Coke.) Therefore, I came to his rescue. I uncharitably happened to bring up Tiananmen Square. "Were you there?" I asked Miles. "No, but my friend was. He was killed." He explained they even interrogated him.

Shino seemed to enjoy this intramural squabble between the two Chinese. He added fuel to the fire when, looking at me, he remarked, "I'm glad we live in democracies." This surprised me coming from Shino, one not given to foment disagreements between the two. There was a slight and, I must say unusual, air of superiority in his comment.

This irked Chen. It was time, Chen determined, to redirect the debate from China to the USA. She cleverly navigated around China's internal problems by introducing the unpopular Iraq War. She stared at me and asked incredulously, "You mean you voted for Buuussh?" as though I had momentarily lost my mind, which in retrospect perhaps I had. She triumphantly took another sip of scotch.

"Well, at least they *can* vote," said Miles, reversing the war of words back to China. "The Communist Party controls everything!" He even remembered something that Mao Tse-Tung had said: "Political power grows out of the barrel of a gun." This stung Chen. "That was then," she said. "It's different now."

Chen felt Miles had overstated the case against the Communist Party. To prove that the party was not filled with evil men, she lowered her voice and said, somewhat sheepishly, "My father is member of Communist Party." She made it sound like the Reverend Jesse Jackson had joined the Ku Klux Klan. I was surprised by her sudden frank admission. Then, after a short pause, she said, "But he's good man." "Well, of course he is," we all said in support. "Just because he's a member of the Communist Party doesn't mean he isn't a good man."

He *was* a good man. I met him initially one summer when he visited Chen. Only, Chen had run afoul of the law again. She was stuck in Toronto at a conference. Because of some self-inflicted problem with her visa, her immediate return to the USA was prohibited. Frantically, she phoned me if I would spend some time with her father in Grand Rapids. I did. I showed him around town. At our place, he presented us with gifts, grateful for our past assistance to Chen. I agreed to help him with his English and promised to send him our ESL book 7, the one we used in class, when he returned to China.

When he revisited Grand Rapids a summer later, I met with him in the apartment Chen had by then rented for the book 7 lessons. He would meet me at my car, carry my books to the entrance he opened for me like my personal valet, lead me into the room by a chair that was strategically positioned before slippers readied for me, had grapes, imported Chinese peanuts, and tea prepared on a table.

After each session, he insisted on carrying my books to the car and surrendered them only after I was comfortably seated behind the wheel. When his wife's visit that summer overlapped with his, we had them over for an evening. They came laden with gifts from China: a splendid shirt for me, fancy shoes for Gertraud, a box of tea, an exquisite calendar splashed with Chinese characters, an illustrated book on Shanghai, an ornate bottle of powerful liquor, which started a fire in my stomach.

Were we to think they were some of these wily Chinese communists, some whom we were earlier warned not to trust, hoodwinking us with gifts. *Oh, please.*

At one time, when I asked him about China, he said, "We need some reforms." "Reforms? What kind of reforms?" I expected he'd list some economic reforms.

"We need to be allowed to speak out our opinions different from that of governmental bad sayings," he said.

This coming from a lifelong member of the Communist Party!

But I have gotten ahead of my story. Miles had cleaned up the dishes and glasses before they left. Gertraud smilingly fingered Chen's empty scotch glass. Laughing, she said, "My, how your classes have improved Chen's English." I did not feel complimented! Partly because my mind was preoccupied with that "it" Shino said Miles "didn't get."

Unfolding Shino's "It"

Shino, I've said, was my Pool. Submerged beneath that smooth and untroubled surface, I suspected some sort of Christianity was swimming around, something like a silvery sunfish. It had not as yet slipped to the top and exposed itself. I wanted to sink my line in to hook that fish, that "it," and bring it out in the open. Nevertheless, I let it alone to allow Shino do his own fishing. Maybe he himself would lift it to the surface, unhook it, and tell us what he meant by his "it." Over the next month or so, during three different events, several things floated to the top that encouraged my suspicion.

You're thinking, "Why didn't you ask him that evening, 'What did you mean by "it," Shino?'?" I didn't probably because with Jesus and my Asian friends, I wanted to be more often like a night watchman waiting for the sun to rise than a probing detective. Besides, Miles was in a feisty mood after the Luther film. He'd interrupt any Christ talk with his criticism of religion.

When the Advent season arrived, our first December in ESL, Immanuel planned an Advent-by-candlelight evening and invited its members to host a table for a number of folks. Nothing elaborate. Only dessert and coffee, with Christmas cookies and decorations. The whole idea was to foster fellowship among church members. Kathy, who was in charge, encouraged members to invite friends, especially unchurched ones, to attend. It was a laid-back way to expose them to the church. Gertraud and I volunteered to host a table.

Before our class began, I invited my three to be our guests. Miles declined. Some weak excuse about already being engaged for that evening.

He generally stiff-armed any invitation to attend even a quasi-religious event. Perhaps he suspected that he'd be infected by some spirituality through the process of osmosis.

I told Shino and Chen, who accepted, that entertainment was also included for the evening. "In fact," I said, "if you have something to present, a skit, a song, something like that, Kathy said I should encourage you to offer your talents. How about it? I wish you would."

"Shino can sing," Chen announced. "He has wonderful voice." "You can sing, Shino? Why didn't you say so? What about you, Chen? Want to sing too?" "Probably not. I'm not good singer. Not like Shino." It turned out her claim was right on the mark.

I told Kathy that Shino would sing something or other.

+++

Our table seated eight people, including Shino and Chen. It was a festive evening, with a hundred or so seated around ten decorated tables in the auditorium. People mingled freely from table to table, exchanging greetings. Two things worried me. One, that *not many* members would come by to greet our Asian guests, and they will conclude that these Lutherans are an aloof and unfriendly bunch. Two, that *too many* members would come by to greet our guests a little too exuberantly, and they will wonder why they were being singled out. To join the church? Thankfully, a happy medium was struck, and the evening proceeded without a hitch.

Mahmud was also there, our Lebanese evangelist, with his group of converts. Might he make some missionary advances and our guests would leave in a huff as once before? But he kept his distance.

After dessert, the entertainment began. Mahmud and his group were the first to perform. He introduced each and every member in lengthy detail, and they presented their even more time-consuming song and dance routine.

The hour was getting late. Time was running out when I introduced Shino. People were getting antsy, you can imagine, eager to "get things over with" and go home. I secretly prayed that my erstwhile Pavarotti would keep his song short and sweet.

Think of my surprise when Shino sang the first stanza of "Silent Night." By heart. In Japanese. There was polite applause, which said in effect, "That was wonderful. Thank you. That's all now. We can all go home."

Shino held up his hand like a stop sign to quiet the crowd. He began the second stanza. For some inexplicable reason, probably because of a full moon that night, Chen leaped to the stage to join Shino in song. It is not an understatement to say that Chen's voice added nothing to Shino's. I didn't criticize her singing, not even jokingly. Neither did Gertraud.

Again applause, louder this time, with the same intent. Again, Shino's hand went up to silence the restless gathering. Don't they know there is a third stanza to "Silent Night"?

All in all, the members genuinely appreciated Shino's performance. They told him so in person.

For my part, I was astounded he sang "Silent Night," from memory—in his native tongue. After all, isn't it a Christian song? I asked him when and where and how he learned it and why. I wanted him to say something like, "From missionaries when I became a Christian back home." "Good," I would then answer. "Now let's talk about Jesus."

It was no such thing. I wasn't even close. Christmas was a secular day in Japan, like Americans observe July 4, though some exchanged gifts, sent cards, decorated Christmas trees, and sang "Silent Night." I was left hanging by what his "it" meant.

Nevertheless, the way Shino sang sincerely from the heart, you couldn't blame me for thinking that there was more Christianity in that Pool than what meets the eye.

+++

I can't help but notice the body language of worshipers when I preach: a woman rolls her eyes and whispers to her husband after every five sentences or so, another critic avoids eye contact and gazes at the ceiling feigning boredom, another yawns by design every three minutes while leafing aimlessly through a hymnal on his lap, another fulfilling a tired habit slouches down in the last seat in the back row. A teenager, who cannot miss a single second of football on TV, gives me that when-will-he-be-finished look.

It's body language announcing that they are not a bit interested in what I'm saying.

But not Shino.

With his eyes fastened on me like a laser beam, he sat there three rows from the front like a devout monk, sopping up everything I said with all ears. This was not a Nicodemus attending worship out of idle curiosity, complimenting me by his presence, "come to see me work." I added this evidence to his "Silent Night." I concluded that this looks much more like a pious Christian at work.

And then he ruined everything, I have to say in a way, when he knelt before me at the Communion rail to receive the Lord's Supper. It was an Advent Sunday worship service, and I was in charge of administering the sacrament.

Now, I'm not a great theologian (except after a Manhattan or two). Still, even I know we don't commune people willy-nilly if they have not passed some necessary signposts along the way. They need to confess faith in the Lord Jesus. (Had Shino done that?) They need to be baptized. (Was Shino baptized?) They need to recognize Christ's presence in the bread and wine. (Did Shino acknowledge that?) And in our circles, you should be, at a minimum, a member of the Lutheran Church. (I knew he wasn't.) I had no hard evidence he met the "qualifications."

I was in a fix. I heard a thousand conservative voices accusing me of heretical practice if I communed him. He had knelt and prayed and sang like all the rest, as though those were the most natural things to do, had heard the Words of Institution. Was that enough? Well. What to do? I couldn't see myself pass him by as though he were a leper. Maybe, I hoped, he just traipsed behind the line coming forward, following the usher's directive, with no real intent to commune, embarrassed to remain behind seated alone.

I whispered to him, "Shino, do you really want to do this?" hoping he'd say no and I'd be left off the hook. Without lifting his bowed head, he nodded yes.

I communed him. To this day, what I did bothers me.

I was consoled later by a friend who told me, "This was no time and place to have a theological discussion, to run through the catechism with him."

He slipped out the back door before we could talk. I could feel my suspicion about what his "it" meant was gaining momentum.

+++

I had never ever arrived late for our ESL classes. A traffic jam delayed me this time, and I was a few minutes late. I found the three already seated. Miles was directing pairings for the Christmas party that Van Andel planned for next weekend. Since each of them could invite a guest, "I'll bring Lin," said Miles, the group's social secretary. "Chen, you invite Gertraud. Shino, you bring Paul." Once again, Miles was dictating assignments, expecting them to comply, which they did.

Miles guaranteed a delightful party, a grand affair, with all the scientists there together with the secretaries, other employees, and the Van Andel "bigwigs." Sounded tempting. So I gladly accepted.

When I told Gertraud about it, she said, "But I don't have a *thing to wear*." On the phone with Chen, Gertraud described what possible meager apparel she might have for this august occasion. "You'll look great," Chen reassured. "Not to worry."

The group, a little more than a hundred, partied in that long, broad hallway on Van Andel's second floor. Guests were milling around with one another in the merry Christmas spirit, relaxed and relieved to be off work, the kind of feeling that you're in the first day of a vacation. Christmas decorations festooned the place. There were six long serving tables, three on either side. One table held Japanese specialties, another Chinese delicacies, the others shrimp, meatballs wrapped in bacon, and other choice offerings.

I had skipped supper at home. I needed to compensate for the lost calories by frequent visits to each table.

I couldn't connect with Miles to thank him for inviting us because he was nowhere to be seen. Or rather, he was everywhere to be seen, flitting like a bumblebee from one person to another, hard to pin down, the life of the party.

Chen introduced Gertraud to the wives of the institute's officials. Gertraud felt ill at ease while this "upper class" exchanged the obligatory compliments. Where *did* you get that dress? What perfect matching shoes! You *must* give me the name of your hairdresser!

At one end of the hall, I saw a large round floor mat, with a five-piece band behind it. Wearied after touring each serving table several times, I sat at a table near where young people were dancing away. The church where I grew up only permitted square dancing. None of this cheek-to-cheek business. Not that's how any of them were dancing tonight. They were doing their modern thing, arms flailing up and down, heads jerking back and forth. I was relieved Chen or Lin didn't insist that I join them in their gyrations—as though they would embarrass themselves by dancing with this old body. For heaven's sake, what was I worried about?

In time, Shino sidled up to me, with two other Chinese, Mei and Lu Sung, on the other side. The three gave one another such knowing glances that I sensed something was up. After some idle chatter, Shino gathered up his courage, as though he were about to ask me for my life's savings. He asked, "I wonder, Paul, if you have the time one of these days, would you tell us more about Jesus?"

So! Finally! That was Shino's "it." Not *about* Jesus. But *more* about Jesus. He simply wanted me to fill in the blanks, he was saying, of a faith in Jesus that was unfinished and incomplete.

"Would I? Certainly I would." We arranged a time and place after Christmas.

+++

What I didn't know *about* Shino was this: Early Sunday mornings he had attended a little Baptist church down the street from Immanuel. Ever since he arrived in Grand Rapids, he attended there for worship and a Bible class. It was there, he told me, he took hold of Jesus. Or rather, Jesus took hold of him. I am ashamed to admit how jealous I was that he connected first with

the Baptists. "Why not with us Lutherans?" I inwardly murmured. I think
I heard a voice answer, "Whether you or they, what does it matter?"

Honestly, how green with envy can you get?

The fact is, it was that Baptist scientist he met in England years ago
and had given him a copy of John's Gospel who influenced him to visit that
Baptist church.

So much of what Shino heard in those Bible classes was more than his
English could absorb at the time, he informed me. Too much living water
for his pool to hold. Then, too, Shino was reluctant to interrupt the class
with questions. There were so many empty spaces in his picture of Jesus
that needed filling in.

For Mei, the Jesus story was a blank page since she was starting from
scratch. Therefore, we spent several weeks in the New Year discussing
elementary details they asked about: names of the disciples, a time line of
events in the first century, the books of the New Testament. "These four
are the Gospels," I pointed out. "The others are writings of various church
leaders." I avoided questions that scholars debate about, the timing of New
Testament events and authorship of its writings. I tried to interject some
humor. "The Sadducees didn't believe in immortality," I said, "that's why
they were *sad-you-see*." Their only response to my hilarious witticism was,
"What did you say?" "Never mind. Skip that," I said.

I soon learned that Lu Sung was already a baptized Christian. Tapping
the top of her head, Chen explained weeks later, "She had the water
sprinkled on her." Lu Sung dropped out of our classes after the first few.
Soon thereafter, she transferred to a clinic in Atlanta. She had established a
bond with her ESL teachers at Immanuel, especially with Kathy, and made
a point of stopping by to say good-bye. I lost contact with Mei after several
months. She spent some time away to adjust some complications with her
visa and then returned to China. That reduced the class, such as it was, to
one. Shino was my sole survivor.

Later, Chen joined us for a few meetings, invited by Shino no doubt.
This didn't completely surprise me. There were some small signs of something
spiritual stirring within her. At any rate, that's what I saw, or wanted to see,
when she signed her Christmas card and e-mails with "God bless you,"

as did Shino. With Miles, it was always, and only, "best regards." On one occasion, before flying to Shanghai for a short visit, she asked, "Paul, will you pray for me?" "You know, Chen, you can pray to God yourself." "But you're closer to God," she said. (I don't know how many times I've heard that, as though we ministers have a special hotline to God.) "I didn't know I was that tall," I said. "You know what I mean, Paul." "Well, OK then, I'll pray for you if you pray for me."

A picture is worth a thousand words, I remembered when I met with Chen and Shino. Why not show them my three videos from *Reader's Digest* on the life of Jesus? I had used them with some small success with my college students. I'm not sure they did much for Chen. And Shino wanted more than that by now. He wanted some sessions devoted to an in-depth study of the teachings of Christianity. The start of those sessions was delayed when I was almost killed.

A Lapsed Memory

All I heard—and felt—was a thunderous crash on the driver's side of our Buick Skylark. It hit me right out of the blue, like a Muhammad Ali knockout punch.

My next conscious moment was when I was slumped, dazed, over the steering wheel. I had exited the shopping center's parking lot on to Twenty-eighth Street after finishing a bowl of chili in a small restaurant called Pal's. The car was smacked westward a hundred feet from the exit and landed in front of Fifth Third Bank. The motor was dead. The front end was a mangled piece of wreckage.

"Paul," an officer asked, "what day is it?" He found my name on my driver's license lifted from my wallet. He was testing how badly my brains were scrambled.

I thought for a few seconds. "It's Monday," I said, "Monday."

"Good," he said as in congratulations. "Now be careful. Don't move your neck."

Others lifted me gingerly from my seat on to a stretcher, which they slipped into a waiting ambulance.

I managed a side-glance across the street where a damaged Mercedes had settled, its two passengers standing, unharmed it appeared, watching if I emerged from our Buick alive. Maybe they were worried they had killed me.

"Are *they* all right?" I asked. (Why was *I* concerned about *them*? For a split second did I imagine *I* was responsible? No, that can't be. I dismissed the thought.)

"They're OK," someone said.

The ambulance, lights flashing, raced off for the hospital. My leg throbbed with pain. So did my head. I asked the female attendant, who held the stretcher in place as the driver swerved in and out of traffic, "Did I suffer a heart attack?" She sounded annoyed. "Don't worry, you'd know if you had a heart attack," she answered as though to say, "Quit whimpering. It's no big deal."

The emergency room performed various tests. X-rays revealed a broken leg bone, the smaller one on my left leg. Also, someone said, "I probably had a slight concussion."

"What, no heart attack?" I demanded of the technician.

"Nope, nothing like that."

"But that's why I crashed."

"No, no sign of a heart attack," he said calmly but firmly.

"I must have. I passed out, lost control, wandered into traffic," I insisted.

"Please, sir, *you had no heart attack*!"

"Can't you see," I said, glaring at the technician, "I couldn't help it. It wasn't my fault! *I had a heart attack!*"

"All right, all right, if you say so," he said condescendingly.

I phoned Gertraud, exaggerating my injury. Worried sick, she rushed to the hospital and, when I was released later that afternoon, took me home.

The next day, I e-mailed my ESL class, detailing the accident and cancelling class for Thursday. Within fifteen minutes, Shino and Chen each e-mailed me. Their messages—I'm summarizing—expressed their typical concern. "What happened? I hope you're not badly hurt. Of course, we must cancel class. You must rest and get well."

Miles, however, went the second mile and phoned. "Paul, I hope you are all right. Is there anything I can do? Should I come to see you?"

That was Miles for you, the ever-helpful Bumblebee. He'd come and offer his considerable expert medical advice.

My doctor does not make house calls. I'm thinking of switching to Miles.

It irritated me that the police did not inform me where they took our car. I phoned the sheriff's office. "It's in the lot across town," I was told, where they deposit wrecked cars. Gertraud drove us there, where we discovered among all the other wreckage our beloved Buick. Gertraud was in love with that Buick. She had purchased it with monies inherited from her father. She was convinced it could be repaired.

"You mean," I joked, "with a little Elmer's Glue and Scotch Tape?"

"It's totaled," the mechanic said. "You'll get some money back—for a tire or two, maybe some other parts—but it's totaled."

Gertraud still insisted we were gypped. "They could have fixed it," she said. "It wasn't that badly damaged."

It was clear, however, her cherished Buick had breathed its last.

I received a citation through the mail. All the incriminating evidence was on it. My name was listed as the offender, along with the name and address of the Mercedes's driver—the innocent one—and the name of the witness, a UPS driver. Below was a neatly drawn design of the accident scene, little symbols for the cars involved. Mine was shown pulled out of a narrow side exit near the Pal's restaurant and in front of the oncoming UPS truck and Mercedes, all on the far east side of the Fifth Third Bank. Why didn't they simply stamp GUILTY across my name?

"Wrong," I told Gertraud. "Wrong, wrong, wrong. I had never ever used that side exit," I insisted. I had always exited by the main four-lane corner at the traffic light, just west of Fifth Third. I had never before taken that narrow side exit. That much I knew for certain. The Mercedes had run a red light, I determined after a five-minute scholarly analysis. Cars always do that on Twenty-eighth Street. It's as simple as that—he ran a red light. Not my fault!

Now, I could simply mail in the fine, and that would be the end of it. But I decided against that. I was wronged, as Chen claimed she was months earlier on the interstate. I checked the box, which requested a hearing and mailed it in. A court-appearance date was set for a few months later.

Ever since I retired, I received the same tired response from the medical profession.

When I asked my doctor why I'm getting so little sleep, waking up after only five hours or so, he said, "As you get *older*, you need less sleep."

My lower back gives me so much pain I can sit only in special chairs. Again, I asked, "What could possibly be wrong? Is there some quick fix?" "It's arthritis," my doctor said. "It often happens in *older* people."

My right eye. It keeps watering. And those bags under my eyes. What can I do about it? I asked my ophthalmologist about it. "It's *old* age. There's nothing much you can do about it."

My dentist wants to take expensive X-rays of my teeth. "Do I really need them?" I asked. "It's best," she tells me. "We need to see your underlying bone structure. It tends to deteriorate as you get *older*."

"I'm having so much stomach pain," I complained to my doctor. "Gertraud thinks it's an ulcer. I'm sure it's cancer." He ordered two CAT scans. Also blood tests. (I already had a colonoscopy.) All tests revealed nothing abnormal. He asked what I have for breakfast. I described a mixture of ingredients our nutrient friend had advised. "You can't eat that concoction anymore," he said. "*Older* people especially need more fiber." It all sounded like a broken record.

I have been known to walk through the rooms in our condo looking for my eyeglasses. "Honey, have you seen them?" I asked Gertraud. "Look in the mirror," she said. "You're wearing them." "Good night! How could I forget! Am I getting Alzheimer's disease?" I asked. "You're getting *old*," she said, confirming the medical experts' demeaning verdict.

I considered the possibility that in my declining years I had forgotten which exit I took at the accident. Did I forget because, after all, I had a brain concussion—and that undetected "heart attack"? Was it actually that narrow side exit the citation described and not the corner with the traffic light I had *always* taken?

In the end, I decided that my bruised brain did not affect my recall. I also rejected the likelihood of a lapsed memory and stuck to my story that the Mercedes ran a red light. Come on, I'm not *that* old.

Besides, I had never gotten into an accident before. Well, yes, I remember that time in Paris with Mike years ago. Just a slight fender bender late at night on a dark street. Hardly what you could call an accident. Anyway, the way the French drive, who could blame me?

I supported my he-ran-a-red-light claim with this charge: *black conspiracy!* In this dark plot, I was aided and abetted by our daughter, up from Chicago for a visit. "Look," she said, noticing the names on the citation. "The driver is a male with a female passenger. They both have different *last* names living at the *same* address. There's some hanky-panky here they don't want exposed in court." Gertraud agreed. It was a closed-and-shut case against them, they both insisted.

It was silly of me, I suppose, but I initially gave their unlikely theory some credence. Was there a cover-up going on here? Was the UPS driver bribed into giving false witness? Did the other driver work out some deal with him? Perhaps they were even related. Was the trooper tricked by them into ticketing me?

I rehearsed this soundproof theory to a friend.

"What's wrong with your family?" he said. "You're a bunch of paranoids!"

"Hold on," I said. "I'm not serious. Just kidding. It's the other two. Honestly, they and their silly suspicions."

Mandana Nakhai

It seemed best to rule out the conspiracy theory. (Although I refused to assign paranoia from my critical friend to each and every single member of our family. *I* am not paranoid.)

What then?

Another theory suggested itself. I've read of accidents caused by careless drivers who had one hand on the wheel and the other on their cell phone. There ought to be a law! Clearly the Mercedes owner ran the red light when distracted while on his cell phone. But I knew I'd have a hard time arguing that in court since he had probably ditched the phone before the trooper arrived.

I felt the evidence for my guiltless pleas crumbling somewhat, similar to how Nixon must have felt during the Watergate hearings. I mulled over which of my more sympathetic friends would provide moral support. I didn't care how biased they'd be in my defense. My ESL friends were odds on favorites.

First, I decided to tease Chen about her accident and subsequent court appearances. I needed some comic relief while I anguished over my predicament.

Now, it's a tricky business in selecting whom to tease. Some people don't have what I call the teasability factor. Some do. My college colleague in New York comes to mind—Mandana Nakhai. She definitely possessed the teasability factor.

Mandana joined our faculty as an English professor. She was an Iranian from an aristocratic family and a brilliant scholar. We knew each other so well partly because her office was in shouting distance from mine just around the corner and down a short hallway. In time she became a close friend of our family, our daughter having majored under her in English. The stories Andrea told me about her class! What a character!

When exasperated by ill-prepared English 101 students, she'd nearly explode. She'd turn her back on the class, count slowly to ten, "One . . . two . . . three . . . ," take a deep breath, face the class again, and then, smiling, string out a lengthy "ooookay," and then continue as though they were the sweetest darlings ever enrolled in college. Andrea and her collaborators mimicked her "ooookay" in earshot of Mandana. They got away with it because Mandana took it in good humor, like Dave Letterman laughing at his own jokes. I think she secretly enjoyed the teasing.

In one class, Andrea told me, Mandana became so excited about Hemingway that she gestured wildly for emphasis with *The Old Man and the Sea* in her right hand. The book, fearing for its safety, took leave of her grip, flew across the room, nearly decapitating a student or two, and landed against the wall. Undaunted by the students' snickering, she forced a "what's so funny? Why you're smiling?" stony, straight-faced glare.

Just last week a student called, asking for a pledge to support the college's choir tour. "Do you know Professor Nakhai?" I asked. "*Do I?*" she asked back and giggled and giggled. "I certainly do," she said, still laughing.

I tell you, this woman has a reputation.

Our faculty had adopted an interdisciplinary course. Two faculty members from separate disciplines combined to teach a course for a two-year stretch. I dreaded the moment I'd be asked to participate and have my incompetence exposed to a colleague. Then one day, our academic dean knocked on my office door. I invented every feeble excuse to escape involvement. But he was so persuasive, and such a kind person, I couldn't turn him down. "I'll do it," I said, "if I can choose my partner. How about Mandana Nakhai?" "Great, let's do it," he said. "You two will be a perfect match." We were to mix English with religion, and as it turned out, I do mean mix.

Mandana was just itching to teach the course. "You can't teach English to students without their background in the Bible," she once told me. "There are so many biblical references in English literature."

She had unbounded energy—she'd stay up all night correcting students' papers—and she threw herself into our course. I took advantage of her enthusiasm. She was a whiz on the computer—I was a computer illiterate—and volunteered to type up all our materials on her word processor. She developed one great idea after the other that summer when we—or was it she—prepared the course. What great fun we had!

She was one of the most good-natured persons I've ever met, which meant I could place her, with malice aforethought, in the teasability factor. She never came to her defense when I complained to my colleagues, "She made me do all the work," another one of my transparent untruths, which, of course, they easily detected. It seems I had a reputation too.

Initially, I was intimidated by Mandana. She had a highfalutin PhD from a prestigious university dangling behind her name. I had only an MA in theology. She never lorded it over me, however, never took advantage of my limited learning. But I took advantage of her. For she had one glaring defect.

She was too short. *Waay too short.* "Be careful when you walk into her office," we warned students, "you might step on her." "I heard that," was all she'd say.

She never retaliated. She always referred to me as Professor Boecler, never simply Paul as I insisted she should. I considered twisting her arm until she'd say Paul. She never did. It wouldn't have worked anyway. She'd suffer a broken arm before she surrendered Professor Boecler. She gave me far too much undeserved respect.

What she lacked in inches above her was replaced in other areas. She'd go on crash diets, which failed her. "Maybe you should lay off those chocolates you've hidden in your office," I timidly suggested. She couldn't see the harm in them. I came to her unsolicited assistance by undermining her hushed-up habit. I devoured as many of them for her as I could when I sneaked into her office and found them secreted under piles of paper. Her office was generally a mess.

She was sipping iced tea at a party I attended. I claimed it was scotch, which, in fact, I knew she hated. I nastily insisted it *was* scotch and that it was adding hundreds of calories to her weight. "Look," she said, holding her glass in front of everyone. *"It's iced tea!"* "Yeah, sure," I said. "It looks to me like you slipped a little scotch in it." She should have dumped the full glass over my balding head. She was too good-natured to do that, which, because the way I teased her, was a remarkable attribute.

Our college was a smoke-free campus. She was as obedient to college rules as an indentured slave. I wasn't. I'd smoke a cigar in my office and then announce to students in the hallway, "I wonder where this hideous smell comes from? Ah, I bet Nakhai is smoking in her office again." I wonder now why I took such mean advantage of her teasability then. I suppose it was because I had missed several appointments with my psychiatrist.

Like I said, she was *waay* too short. She would show videos in class. Trouble was she couldn't reach the screen all rolled up over the blackboard to pull it down. "Professor Boecler, I need your help. Would you reach up to the handle?" I was tempted to say, "A little too short, are you?" That would be pushing the teasing too far, don't you think? But when we turned the lights off after class, I admit I did say, "Let me. I can reach the light switch," which was on the wall adjacent to the doorknob. She murmured, "One of these days . . ." which was about as much of a threat as she could mount. She never once embarrassed me when I garbled my grammar in class or made a howler of a spelling mistake.

I'd hold my head at eye level, looking all over the room when class began, and ask, "Has anyone seen Prof. Nakhai? . . . Oh, there you are," looking down on her at my side. I was nothing but awful with Mandana, just terrible. I could not believe she didn't just simply belt me one. I couldn't help myself, though. She just had too much teasability in her—that's all that's to it.

Mandana was absolutely meticulous about writing correct English. Misspellings, grammatical boners, syntactical foul-ups, punctuation errors—all but horrified her when they made their ugly appearances on students' papers. In addition, "Their papers must look pleasing to the eye," she told me when we prepared directions for students' submissions in our interdisciplinary course. Therefore, proper formatting was important, she insisted, which included correct indenting and spacing between paragraphs where required.

Ever since I retired, I've missed seeing her react to unforgivable gross blunders of the English language. With a heavy sigh, and I suspect a broken heart, she'd get out her marker and circle the transgression on the students' papers. I've missed sitting in her office, sharing secrets, stories, and some chocolates. And yes, let's be honest, I've missed the opportunity of teasing her, just a tiny bit, just enough to elicit a "now, Professor Boecler . . ."

What good fortune I had when a few years ago, I had an opening to renew my evil habit and provoke Mandana's agitation over incorrect English.

Concordia College had announced an opening in the English Department. The applicant should possess a terminal degree, be willing to teach courses in the core curriculum, advise students, and so on. All applications were to be addressed to Dr. Mandana Nakhai, head of the English Department. With my family's collaboration, I concocted this letter and—to throw her off my track—had a neighbor sign it and mailed it from another city other than Grand Rapids. It read as follows:

Dr. Mandana Nakhai
171 White Plain Road
Concordia College
Bronxville, NY 10708

Dear Madonna,

I am herewith applying for the full time position in English and composition at Concordia College, New York, as announced in the August 23, 2005 issue of the Lutheran Witness. It would be a great honor to work side by side with you in facilitating students to actualize their potential efficacy in mastery elegant English and Rhetoric. I am confidant that us two would make a great team.

I am presently terminating my degree in English, writing or Rhetoric and am therefore eager to launch my career, "with white sails flying," in a college just like yours'. I am also desireable in specializing in secondary English education. My companion and myself, in addition to teaching, will assist me in advising students.

I also desire to acquire to the core of things in life rather than to allocate my days to the periphery of earthy existence and so there fore because of that I would be a good fit at your core curriculum. I also am fond of surveying literatures; and modesty speaking I am good at speaking.

I also do all my instruction in the classroom for both upper and lower courses.

Myself, I also like to travel broadly as you yourselves can deduct from the names listed below in the References who I have visited which the information of one of those listed is not acquired which I will do as soon as I get my typewriter fixed. (it is broke) That means that I have attained a broad range of subjects which I am fairly familiar with. The vita is also not done due to the fact and because of the afore-mentioned broken typewriter which I will get to you as soon as I have got it done.

Me and my companion, we don't need a lot of money and so there fore we will be satisfied with whatever you will give ourself by way of cash money in the salary.

I leave you with this saying from T. S. Eliot (1888-1965)—

Let us go then, you and I, When the evening is spread out against the sky

Like a patient etherized upon a table.

With fondest regards, and looking forward to meeting you soon, I am

Cincerely Yours,

Anton Emerson Katzen-Pfoten II

references (I empower you to consult them personally in my name!)

1. Miss Ellen McKinley, Sunday School superintendant, First Lutheran Church, 7902 Deer Run Road, Manitoba, Canada.
2. Markus
3. Prof. Dr. Chao-Bei Qian, M.A., MDHP, PhD, Peking Medical University, Department of Medical English, 38 Xueyuan Dong, Beijing, China. Office: 86-01-10925483 Home: 86-01-65982376

When Mandana opened and read my letter, they told me the building where her office was located *trembled and shook.*

A Foiled Attempt at Teasing

I selected Chen for the teasability factor by the process of elimination.

I could never bring myself to tease Shino. I can't exactly say why. It wasn't because he was so straight-faced that he couldn't enjoy a joke or that he'd get sensitive when Miles wisecracked about some peculiar Japanese trait. I suppose it's because I drew a circle of respectability around him and could not cross over the line. He had that regal, imperial look about him, something like a sacred Rembrandt painting in a museum you admired from a distance. I'm sure he never ate anything with calories in it, which meant he was thin, so thin that you'd miss him if you looked at him sideways. Yet I'd never teased him about that any more than you'd tease Saint Francis for feeding his birds. Besides, how can you tease anyone who loved scotch?

Miles, on the other hand, was born to be teased. God created him that way. He had so many eccentricities that demanded some ribbing: his unsolicited "wisdom" bestowed on one and all, that round, full face with its impish smile, his breathless energy that left us sucking for air when he was leading the way to wherever. And then there was that confident agnosticism in matters religious "where angels feared to tread."

When we first met, he told me he had moved early on from Thailand to China. Whenever I introduced him to friends, I explained that he left Thailand because the CIA was after him as a terrorist. He'd laughingly and patiently correct me each and every time I deliberately repeated it. "Ah, that's right," I'd innocently say. "I forgot. Now I remember." I had already teased him so often that it began to wear thin. So I eliminated him this time. Enough was enough.

There were several reasons why I settled on Chen. I couldn't pick on her for being short as I could with Mandana. Nor did she have any of Miles's eccentricities. But she possessed the same good-natured qualities, as when she simply brushed off my previous spoofing of her driving habits. That was a good sign that she wouldn't fly off the handle if I needled her about her own accident. After all, she had escaped a ticket at court by a technicality although she had insisted, "It wasn't my fault." That made her vulnerable for my ribbing. And what with her "innocent" run-ins with the law, perhaps I'd get some sympathetic understanding for my own plight.

It all backfired. Instead, we got into an argument.

Here's how it happened. We were having another pizza party, and I mentioned my accident to Chen. First, I tried to elicit some sympathy.

"Chen, that accident I got into? Guess what? They blame me for it."

"Well, there must be reason. What did you do?"

"What did I do? I didn't do anything."

"Must be something. Where was accident? Maybe you drive too fast."

"I was hardly moving at all. It was at a four-lane intersection. I was slowly moving into it."

"Did you look both ways first?" she asked, interrogating me.

"I didn't have to. There's a traffic signal there."

"When you go on to street, was light green?"

"Of course, it was green. Why would I start in if it wasn't green?"

"Maybe light was still yellow. Were you in hurry?"

"I'm retired, Chen! I'm never in a hurry. Don't have to be."

"You should still look both ways. Must always be careful," she said like a reprimand.

"Anyway, the point is, they blame me!" I persisted.

"Isn't that too bad? I get blamed too, you know."

"I'm trying to tell you, it wasn't my fault."

"So?" she said, indifferently. "They blamed me when it wasn't my fault."

This was not precisely the sympathetic response I expected from my graceful Swan.

I retaliated.

"As I recall, it was clearly established you were to blame. You made an illegal U-turn."

"Not then. Other time. On interstate. My Toyota was totaled."

"You were going too fast then. That's why."

"What too fast?"

"You must have. You ignored the speed limit before."

"I was *not* too fast. I was cut off. I told judge that. She let me go."

"That's not what the judge said. I was there, you know."

"She didn't say I was guilty," she said, defensively.

"That's because she let you off on a technicality, that's why."

"What technicality?"

"The trooper didn't show up in court. He couldn't press charges. You were let off."

"She would have anyway if I had chance to explain. You rushed me out of room."

Maybe Chen was uncharacteristically in a bad mood that evening. Maybe there was a full moon again. Somehow it was all my fault. I had hoped she'd support my position, sympathize with my predicament. Instead, I got blamed for hers.

I changed the mood by trying to pull her leg a little.

"Maybe I'll get off on a technicality too. Maybe the officer who ticketed me would suddenly contract leprosy on the way to court and couldn't appear."

"Very possible. Common disease in Grand Rapids," she said with a straight face.

"No, it could happen. I'm serious."

"So am I. Really," she said. "I see many people on streets with leprosy every day."

"They'd have to quarantine him on the other side of the state," I said.

"His wife will divorce him then," she said as she forced back a smile. "That's what he gets for awful thing he did to you."

"It would only be the twenty-four-hour type. He'd get over it with an aspirin or two."

"Just be sure it's Tylenol," she said.

"You don't believe me, do you?"

"I do. I do. I always believe, Paul."

Chen just shook her head in amused annoyance. She had turned the tables on me. Her leg didn't budge an inch when I pulled it. I learned there and then that assigning people to the teasability factor was not an exact science.

Asian Athleticism and Geometry

Miles and Shino had stood in the background all this time, snickering, amused by our absurd dialogue. I declared an armistice between the two of us and invited them all to our condo's lower level. Miles stayed topside. It agitates Miles whenever he sees someone in dire straights. And Gertraud was in dire straights because she cannot tolerate leaving behind a "mess."

My dictionary defines a "mess" as a confused, dirty, or offensive state. Gertraud defines a "mess" as five soiled pizza dishes and glasses left standing in the kitchen sink. A "mess" is also a cookie crumb I've dropped on the kitchen floor. This is a serious health hazard because it will attract a swarm of ants or a stray dog. Gertraud is one of these housewives who clean the windows before the hired window washers arrive. "What will they think if they see dirty spots on them?"

At one end of the long lower level stood an elliptical machine. We had purchased it on sale. I planned to get my exercise on it especially during the winter months. "Do you use it much?" Shino asked me. "Not really. It's too difficult to operate. I need to adjust its controls but don't know how. I've meant to call the store for directions. The pedals just don't run smoothly enough. It kills my legs whenever I've tried it."

"May I try?" Shino asked. "Sure. Why not? Be careful not to hurt yourself."

Hurt himself? He leaped on to it like a bunny, and his feet flew across the pedals. He seemed to be walking on thin air. This continued for five to ten minutes. He smiled at me all the while with that "see!" look on his face, you know, the kind that says triumphantly, "Look at me. What's so tough about this?" While it's not like Shino to rub it in, I, at any rate, took personally the ease with which his feet manipulated this impossible elliptical, as though our cultures were competing with each other. Although I am not paranoid, I suspected a designed and deliberate exhibition of Asian physical superiority. *Wait a minute,* I thought, *he's forty-some years younger than I am. If I were his age, I'd . . . well, maybe not.* I tried to look unimpressed, but was I ever relieved when he *finally* dismounted.

"Are you all right?" I asked, certain he'd have to pause, gasping for air, trying to catch his breath. It pains me to report there was no panting, no huffing and puffing. He simply looked at me quizzically. You could tell he was thinking, "What's wrong with Paul? Why does he ask?"

Just then, Miles, his Good Samaritan mission accomplished, bounded into the room and joined Shino at the Ping-Pong table. It was a surprise gift from our son, Gerhardt, and his wife, Lynn, when we first moved to Grand Rapids. They transported it all the way from Chicago on their SUV, unpacked it, carried it by sections downstairs, and set it up in the center of the room. All by themselves. Isn't it nice to have such thoughtful and generous children? No offense to those whose children are otherwise.

I hope it's not bragging when I say that I have always thought of myself as a rather accomplished Ping-Pong player. I have enjoyed my full measure of success at the table. For instance, my son, Gerhardt, and I had played Ping-Pong dozens of times in our basement in New York. I had bested him perhaps 90 percent of the time. I admit he was only an eighth grader then. Still, a win is a win.

My ego was summarily deflated when I sat with Chen on a short bench and watched Miles and Shino go at it with a Ping-Pong match. My jaw dropped, shocked and amazed. I bet the Chinese had invented Ping-Pong along with gun powder a thousand years ago, and Miles must have been practicing ever since. The same for Shino. Aren't these brilliant scientists supposed to be intellectual eggheads, clumsily uncoordinated in sports? Well, that's not what I saw. In fact, it's not possible for me to describe what I saw.

With that in mind, when Miles invited me for a match, I looked for a way out. I visualized what it would be like competing with Miles, like playing tennis with Roger Federer or matching strokes with Tiger Woods. I may have been born at night, like Lee Trevino said, but it wasn't last night. I pointed to my broken leg bone, which in all truth had been pretty well healed by then. "It incapacitates me from playing," I told Miles. He bought it. He probably did not know what "incapacitates" means. One embarrassing scene of Shino on that "inoperable" elliptical was enough.

Miles joined Chen and me on the bench. I pulled out an aerial view of the accident scene, which I had xeroxed at the county office. We stretched it out on the Ping-Pong table. "I don't know," I confessed, "maybe they're correct. Here is where the demolished Buick landed," I pointed out. "Here is the big intersection where I claim I exited. If I did exit there, how could the Buick end up here?" I drew an *X* at the spot. "Maybe I *did* take that side exit they said. Can't remember. You know, I think they've got me."

"Not at all," Miles said. "This is what you do. Use geometry." He drew a right angle over the scene, one horizontal line connecting the two exits, the other a vertical one connecting the side exit with where the Mercedes landed on the other side of the street. Then he finished the triangle with another line. "We call that hypotenuse," he said. I felt insulted. "I *know* what a hypotenuse is," I answered. "If you see where Buick landed compared to where Mercedes was, it's impossible you took side exit. Show that to judge," Miles said, satisfied with his incontrovertible proof.

I had no idea what he meant. Perhaps I needed to review my high school geometry course. Still it seemed to me it proved nothing. Even Shino was puzzled by the diagram. The more Miles explained, the more I questioned my own claim. I knew the judge wouldn't buy Miles's triangle, hypotenuse and all. Miles was overtaxing his knows-everything into a contorted effort to take my side, it seemed to me.

I told them, "I still think . . . I'm almost sure, I had taken the traffic signal exit." I was wavering because of that incriminating evidence on the citation. It gnawed at me. I began to feel like some lines in *The King and I*:

> There are times I almost think
> I am not sure of what I absolutely know.
> Very often find confusion
> In conclusion I concluded long ago . . . .

In my head are many facts
of which I wish I was more certain I was sure!
. . . a puzzlement.

Still, I decided as a last resort to stick to my shaky story.

We finally called it quits for the evening. Before they left, Chen gave me the best advice of all. "Remember to do one thing," she advised. "What's that?" "Be sure to wear your clerical collar to court. You know how that helps." I thought I detected the merest hint of sarcasm in her advice. "Good idea," I said. "And take Gertraud with you," she added.

Courtrooms and Clerical Collars

I still don't know my way around Grand Rapids very well. I mostly follow a beaten path to places I regularly frequent—the bank, the supermarket, our church, the doctor's office, places I need to go. I've certainly never needed to go to the courthouse. I didn't want to arrive late for the hearing and keep the judge waiting. Judges hate that. Ask Paris Hilton. I looked up the address, made a dry run, and memorized the way.

I had never been in a courthouse before. Once, it's true, I was—long ago. When I lived in Cincinnati, a recent graduate of the seminary, I had been ticketed for crossing a yellow line while driving through a neighboring village. I knew I was guilty and went a few days later to pay the fine at the village office.

You can hardly call it a courthouse. I entered a tiny room, and just one man, probably the village mayor, sat behind a small desk. He asked to see my license. My name on it did not include my title, reverend. When he asked about my occupation, he said, "I'm sorry. Why didn't you tell the officer when you got the ticket? Your name with title will appear in the traffic violation section of our weekly newspaper. We don't like to embarrass the clergy. Maybe I should just forgive the fine." "Well, I broke the law, and I should pay the fine." I was so guileless those days, so honest and straightforward. He reluctantly accepted my check.

So there. See, I didn't always try to circumvent the law as a man of the cloth. (But I did make sure my title was always attached to my name when I renewed my license.)

However, in this case years later in Grand Rapids, when I was obviously "innocent," I took Chen's advice and felt justified in using my clerical collar to my advantage.

On the day of the hearing, Gertraud and I announced ourselves and were ushered into a small room near the entrance. I was relieved they did not take us to the large courtroom, a few yards down the hallway and off to the right. There, apparently, they tried high crimes and serious felonies: serial killers, extortioners, and mass murderers. I assumed they reserved this small room for simple cases like mine, which might be easily dispensed with once they heard my side of the story.

The judge sat in shirtsleeves behind a desk, his back to a wall of shelves filled with legal documents. He looked bored, even annoyed by this "fellow" challenging a cut-and-dried case. You could tell he was thinking, "Why fritter away my time and the trooper's with this hearing. He could be out enforcing the law. A waste of the taxpayer's money."

I sat off to the side by a window, Gertraud next to me. I wore my black preacher's suit, black shirt, black shoes, black socks. By way of contrast, this made my shiny white clerical collar conspicuous, like a halo, I hoped. I had "clergyman" written all over me. This was my deliberate plan. More like a plot, a scheme, I confess.

Gertraud was fidgeting in her chair, itching to begin with an opening statement. Gertraud becomes absolutely furious when she perceives any injustice perpetrated against one of her own, her son, her daughter, even me. Years ago when Gerhardt was a youngster and we had just moved to New York, one of his new nasty playmates called him a Nazi, aware that his mother was a German. She was ready to march right over to the kid's parents and reprimand them for having reared such an awful child but restrained herself.

C. S. Lewis once asked, "If your dog has bitten the child next door, . . . which would you sooner have to deal with, the master of that house or the mistress?" His clear inference was you would fear the mother most. Gertraud was like that. Only now, I was her child, and she was ready to give the court a piece of her mind in my defense. "Please, honey," I whispered, "not now. Not now."

The first hearing had been postponed till now because the arresting trooper was on vacation. When he didn't appear today when we were about to begin, I felt a tingle of hope that I'd have the same good fortune as Chen's. I knew leprosy was out of the question, but maybe his way to court was aborted by an emergency call to chase down some robbers or investigate a domestic violence disturbance. In another fifteen minutes, the judge would need to dismiss the case. I'd be a free man. No such luck. The judge dashed my hopes by announcing, "He's called ahead. He'll be a few minutes late."

When he finally arrived, he quickly took his seat by the door on the opposite side of the room. Not once did he glance over to our side. An air of confidence permeated his posture, straight up and erect. Not a hint in his demeanor that he had ticketed the wrong driver. I took this as a bad sign. He didn't speak a word. He didn't have to. His face said impatiently, "Such a clear-cut case. Let's get this over with. I have to get back to work."

My, was he handsome—young and clean shaven and tall and blond. Not like one of those potbellied policemen I saw sometimes in New York City. He looked Dutch. There are so many with Dutch heritage in our area that the saying around here was, "If you're not Dutch, you're not much." We noticed the difference when we moved from New York where many in our neighborhood were short with a swarthy complexion. The Dutch here were tall and blond. Added to that was the claim, as we were told, "The Dutch here are so honest." I was not encouraged when I mulled this over. Another bad sign.

I don't think he was out of his twenties. His pants and shirt were squeaky clean, spotless, all the creases of his uniform pressed razor sharp that you could cut your finger on them. He appeared so authoritative, so in command, like the head of the FBI. I knew he couldn't have been on drugs when he arrived at the accident scene.

The judge reviewed the citation and routinely looked over the entries in a matter-of-fact manner. I expected he'd ask for my version, which I had been rehearsing (omitting reference to Miles's hypotenuse), but he seemed to feel "why bother?" Without looking up, only occasionally glancing sideways at me, he'd ask, "Your name is? . . . Your address? . . . Make of car?" He addressed me, at one of his side glances, with "mister" and then, later, "sir." (What's wrong with the man, can't he see? Is he color-blind? Does he have it in for the clergy? Cut me some slack, man, I'm a man of the cloth.) Then he felt obliged to correct himself and said, "I don't mean to sound disrespectful. What should I call you? Is it reverend?" "It doesn't matter," I answered. "No, no, you can call me anything," I answered as though I hadn't worn the clerical collar to influence his decision. "I'm not fussy about titles, Your Honor. Stick to mister if you like."

I hope you're not thinking, *What a hypocrite!*

The whole affair took a mere fifteen minutes or so, and the judge was about to announce the fine. The trooper came to my partial defense, although belatedly, when he told the judge, "His view of the Mercedes was blocked by the UPS truck." (Why didn't he announce that earlier?) It didn't matter. This irritated the judge, and he brushed aside the comment as though to say, "Sorry, that's beside the point." Then he looked at the citation again, this time studied it. Some entry at the top caught his eye. It puzzled him. I whispered to Gertraud, "Uh-oh, now what? Am I in still deeper trouble now?"

He suddenly whirled around in his chair, reached for a large volume on the wall of his books, opened it, and turned to some page. He frowned at the trooper and said curtly, "You've entered the wrong code number. Case dismissed." Just like that. I was free to go. Off, like Chen, on a technicality.

However, apparently annoyed that I had gotten off the hook and to even the score, he admonished me, as though I were a schoolboy, "If the insurance companies take this to a trial, you'll have to plead guilty."

I knew the two of us had the same insurance company, State Farm, and happily told him so as if I had the last word after all. "Uh-huh, I see," he said, "it doesn't matter then."

When we got up to leave, "Just one question," I said. "I was fairly sure the accident was at the main intersection, the one with the traffic signal. How can you tell it was at the side exit?" "Because of the debris the crash left," he said dismissively. "It collected there where the citation noted the accident." "Aha," I said, "I sort of suspected that."

Gertraud and I left the room swiftly just in case the judge discovered something else in his books to reverse his decision.

I could hardly wait to tell Chen and Shino and Miles.

Death and Resurrection

Gertraud doesn't like to think about death very much—or talk about it. I do. Especially mine. I do since I'm fairly convinced that I'll die someday. I talk to her about my death because of the final details involved: funeral service to plan, tombstones and burial plots to purchase, and so forth. Because I'm nine years older than Gertraud and will likely die before she does (our financial planner keeps rubbing that in), I told her, "I don't want to burden you with those last-minute arrangements."

It was on my conscience because my friend Carl Bretscher long ago informed me that his funeral was already paid for, all the procedures for burial taken care of beforehand for the sake of his children. My father had done the same, who followed my mother in death, so that there would be no final rushed arrangements for my sister and me to make. I wanted to do the same for Gertraud.

"I don't want to be left alone," she'd say, "I want to go when you do." "That might be a little difficult to organize," I said, "unless you have a plan in mind." "Don't be silly," she said. "I'm not that desperate."

It was like pulling teeth to get Gertraud to discuss funerals and tombstones and burial plots. It seemed she had enrolled in what someone has called "this great conspiracy of silence." I'm always amused by how some TV reporters announce that someone or other "has passed away," a euphemism for "died." Or as one commentator noted, "They have reached the end point of their natural history."

I sometimes told my college students, "When Boecler dies, say, 'He's dead. Dead as a doornail.'" That may sound morbid, but that's what happens.

Of course, I believe that death is not my final destination. But when I die, "I'm dead," right? Why not use the word?

I finally persuaded Gertraud to think seriously about this because, "It's also not fair for our children," I said. "Think of it. Gerhardt and Andrea live in Chicago. They'd need to come all the way to Grand Rapids when the time comes and be on their own to make last-minute decisions. Because if I die first, you'll be so grief stricken, you'll be unable to assist them. You *will* be grief stricken, won't you? Or not?" "Yes, yes, of course." "If we both die together, say, suddenly in another of my accidents, I'm afraid our kids might make a mess of what to do with us." "Please," Gertraud said. "Don't be silly. Give them some credit."

Eventually, we decided to go to Chicago and find a plot at Saint Luke Cemetery where the Boecler clan is buried. The whole relationship is buried there, the Boecler and Bruckner grandparents, my father, my mother, some other distant relatives. We did it. We drove to Chicago, looked up the cemetery, and bought a plot. They couldn't fit us in next to the relatives but did find a plot a few yards away, next to the side of the road.

Soon after our return from Chicago, I met with my ESL class on our scheduled Thursday evening. *The Passion of the Christ* filmed in our area; it was around Easter that spring. Miles made plans for us to see it. He insisted on it. That surprised me, coming from Miles. I wasn't surprised as much that he wanted to see the Luther film. That one intrigued him because he relished all the history and politics part of it. It was not so specifically spiritual in content as the *Passion* movie was, and what spiritual content there was in the Luther film didn't connect with Miles—or was ignored—that "it" that Shino said "Miles didn't get."

However, he could not have missed the TV news about the *Passion* film, with people shown leaving theaters weeping and others interviewed who were shaken by Christ's suffering. You can appreciate that I was both surprised and pleased that Miles initiated the idea. Maybe Christ's death and Resurrection would lead to some fruitful discussion during our planned pizza party after the movie.

Gertraud begged off accompanying us to the theater. Violent scenes bothered her. That's why we often watch television on separate sets. I prefer movies like *The Godfather*. She chooses the Hallmark Channel and sweet and sentimental programs where no blood is shed or shots fired.

I studied the faces of Chen and Shino and Miles as we left the theater. I wanted to gauge their reaction. Chen said nothing but looked thoughtful, pensive as she passed me. Shino suddenly remarked, "I've seen movie before." "You have?" I asked, surprised. "Yes, this is second time." "Really? You went alone? You should have asked me. I would have come along." "No, no," he said. "I went with group from Baptist church. They invited me to see it with them." "You don't say. With the Baptists? Good for them," I said, disappointed that I had not thought of that first. Miles looked blasé about the experience, as though he had just seen Tom Hanks in *The Da Vinci Code*. An indifferent attitude was written across his face, unmoved by the suffering scenes, seemingly skeptical the claims *The Passion* made about the person of Christ.

I drove home alone after the matinee; the others in Miles's car. I would have loved to have heard them discuss the movie among themselves. Would Shino share his newfound beliefs? Would Miles vent his skepticism? What would Chen say?

I guess I'll never know because when we gathered at our place, no one brought it up. I didn't either, thinking, "Let's see what they say first."

I sat in my favorite chair facing the couch where Miles sat to the right and Chen to the far left. Shino stood lingering around in the back near the kitchen, offering to help Gertraud serve the pizza.

While we were eating, I told them all, "Gertraud and I recently returned from Chicago."

"To visit your children?" Chen asked. "How is Andrea? I really like her." They all had met her on a visit here when we had a pizza party.

"She's fine," I said. "Thanks for asking. So is our son Gerhardt. You've never met him, have you? We really went to Chicago for another reason," I went on. "We're concerned about Andrea and Gerhardt when we die."

"When you die?" asked Chen, incredulously. "You're not that old."

"You think? Look, I'm getting on in years. So is Gertraud. She's old," I said, with a little wink aimed at Gertraud. Gertraud didn't object. "We purchased a burial plot in Chicago. Now our children won't have to search for one when we're gone."

"Why Chicago? Why not in Grand Rapids?" Chen asked. "Like I said," I explained. "We want to spare our children the trip. If we die here in Grand Rapids, the funeral home will ship us to Chicago."

"Shipped? On train? That would cost money."

"Well, yes," I told Chen, "not as much if Gertraud dies first though. We have different opinions about what to do with our corpses. Gertraud wants to be cremated. Then I'd just put her remains in an urn, place it on the backseat of our car, drive her down to Chicago. Saves money. If I die first, we have a friend who'll take Gertraud."

Chen just shook her head at the cavalier way I spoke about our deaths and burials. "We do it different way in China."

"Anyway," I said, "we want Chicago also because all my relatives are buried there. It will be nice to be near them. Gertraud doesn't mind. She doesn't want to be sent all the way back to Germany, do you, honey?" Gertraud nodded.

"So you really bought plot in Chicago?" Chen asked.

"They couldn't find one next to my relatives' graves. Instead, they squeezed us into a plot some distance away, right next to the road. That will make it simpler for our kids too. That way, when they honor us, all they'll have to do is drive by, throw some artificial flowers out the window on to our graves without stopping. It could be raining, you know. Aren't we considerate?"

Chen dropped her jaw in dismay. "Paul, how you talk about these things!"

"When I wrote a thousand-dollar check for the plot, I gave it to the administrator of the cemetery in his office. I asked him, 'If the Lord returns before we die, do we get our money back?' There was a lengthy pause. He gave us a curious, perplexed look. He said, 'You know, I've gotten a lot of questions, but never one like that.' Finally, he had to laugh with us about it."

"How can you joke about something as serious as death?" Chen asked.

"I suppose that sounds callous," I answered. "But if what Gertraud and I believe about the Resurrection—Christ's and ours—as we do, then why can't we laugh, or at least smile, about it sometimes?"

When we finished the pizza, I finally asked, "What about the movie? Any questions?"

Chen was the first to ask, with tears in her voice, "Why did they beat Jesus so much? What wrong did he do?"

"That's what Pilate asked," Shino said. "He thought Jesus was innocent. He had Jesus beaten to satisfy crowd. Pilate still had him killed. But Jesus rose anyway."

"Nice going," I wanted to tell Shino.

All the while Miles was shifting in his seat. The idea of a resurrection was getting to him. It was more than he could take, and he was itching to air his skepticism.

Usually Miles criticized religion in a gradual way, first asking some innocent-sounding questions. Months ago he once asked me, "How do you get paid?"

"I'm retired, Miles. I don't get paid anymore."

"But when you preach sometimes, how much do you charge?"

I knew what he was getting at. I remembered his sarcasm when he told me, "You always have to pay Buddhist priest before they pray for you." He was going to put me in the same category.

"Charge?" I said. "I don't charge anything. I receive what a church decides to give me."

"Really?" he said. He sounded disappointed, as though he found no chink in my armor.

On another occasion, he asked, this time with a slight grin, "Why do Christians make sign of cross? I'd just like to know." "I usually don't cross myself," I said. "Others do it for various reasons."

He mentioned with amusement how athletes sign themselves as they come to bat in baseball or before they shoot a foul shot in basketball. "Why do *they* do it?" he asked suspiciously.

"I don't know. You'll have to ask them."

"Well, I think they do it for good luck. They're superstitious," he said as if he had scored a telling point, as though he had exposed religion's black magic.

"Maybe some are," I agreed. "I know some Christians do it to recall Christ's death on the cross. See the connection? It reminds them to be self-sacrificial as Christ was."

He threw in his towel and left it at that, with some restraint.

That's how Miles often disparaged religion, step by step, beginning with curious questions. At least that's how they appeared at first sight. He was not always blunt when he cross-examined religion.

However, this evening, he relieved himself of his bent-up skepticism when he blurted out from his seat, with full confidence, "They *stole* Christ's body from the grave!"

Now how do you answer that? I remembered all the objections to that claim. Instead I simply said, "The early Christians were convinced of Christ's Resurrection not because the grave was empty, but because they *saw* him—resurrected."

"Aha. Is that so? Really?" he smirked, as though we believed in Santa Claus.

Miles was clearly not finished and took his omniscient freethinking a step further. Like a prosecuting attorney, he asked, "If Jesus was the Son of God, what does that make me, a nephew of God?" He was in total ridicule mode. I remembered what Tom Cahill once wrote, "For those who believe in God, no explanation is necessary. For those who do not, no explanation is possible."

Nevertheless, I answered, "You can do better than that. Jesus is your gift certificate. Cash that in and then you can become a child of God." He looked at me as though I was relating a fairy tale. "If I gave you a thousand dollars instead, would that make me a child of God?"

"Try it," I said.

I really loved Miles. For all his skepticism, you couldn't help loving him. He was so refreshingly honest. It's a shame. He had many outward marks of a Christian: kind, considerate, unselfish, generous. Still, he lacked that One Person whom we might one day persuade him to accept. At this point now, as I told Gertraud when they left, "It's like doing carpentry work on a burning building."

Religion 101

My in-depth study of Christianity with Shino was delayed by my accident and court hearing. About the time of the *Passion* movie and subsequent pizza party, Shino and I got back to his initial request.

We met, he and I, on Tuesday evenings. We met not in the large classroom where the three assembled for ESL, but in a small room just up the stairs off the church's side entrance. It was an intimate setting where Shino and I sat facing each other across a little round table.

I wanted to keep it casual, informal, and to help achieve that atmosphere, I bought some peanuts on my way to church. I spread them out on a napkin in front of Shino. As I helped myself, I said, "Have some, Shino." He took *a* peanut. One, single, solitary peanut between his thumb and forefinger like a thief does when pickpocketing someone's wallet. "Goodness, Shino, take some more. Take a handful." He took two or three more. And that was it. Maybe he didn't like peanuts. More likely, this was Shino's Asian temperament, reserved and restrained, careful not to take advantage of my offer. So much for my peanut approach at informality.

I remembered what a longtime member of our congregation once mentioned. He knew a pastor whose sermons were brilliant. They were erudite, profound, scholarly, rich in theological verbiage, but he told me, "His sermons went right over our heads." I didn't need to worry about being erudite and profound since I am neither.

I resolved to keep my discussion as down-to-earth as possible. I left out all the "-ation" words, like "justification," "sanctification"; the "-logy" terms you find in the doctrinal tomes such as "soteriology" and "eschatology"; I definitely decided against the "omni-" words for God like "omniscient," "omnipotent," "omnipresent" even though God is. On the other hand, I didn't sink so low as to describe God with that denigrating term "the man upstairs." And I never tried to explain the hypostatic union of the Trinity.

I pulled out my wrinkled notes for the Christian faith course I taught at college in New York, selected the teachings most central to the faith, and condensed them into a "crash course" of six weeks or so.

I call it a crash course because the matter was urgent. Shino was returning to Japan in July, three to four months after my accident. To Japan—for good! I hated that. I'd miss him so. Of course, I knew all along that his two-year stay in the USA would end. But I never wanted to think about it. I put it off, just like I put off thinking about the sun burning up in a billion years from now.

I wanted to hang on to Shino. I even hinted that he might like to move to America, wife and kids and all. I must say he seemed to give it some thought. Certainly, his wife would secure a position in Grand Rapids. Still, time had passed, his two sons were thoroughly ensconced in soccer back home, and there would be that problem of their adjusting to our culture. I was grasping at straws, as I usually do when facing an uncomfortable inevitability. No! Shino's return to Japan would be permanent!

What's more, what would this do to my ESL class: this odd but perfect mixture of personalities? Chen, the aristocratic Swan, China all wrapped up in one person; Miles, Who-Knows-Everything, this unpredictable gadfly, whose pronouncements both annoyed and entertained us; Shino, the class's balance wheel, whose mature presence had a stabilizing effect on the class. I needed all three together to make this work for me. So now, what would our class be like—or our pizza parties and moviegoing for that matter— without Shino?

Of course, I'd still have Chen and Miles, although I had the sinking feeling that one or both might be leaving too. Nevertheless, lacking Shino, a special component would be missing, like butter on my popcorn, like riding a tricycle with two wheels. Maybe another Van Andel scientist, perhaps from Japan, might fill Shino's void. Could a newcomer ever possibly be a substitute for Shino this late in the game? Without Shino, it wouldn't be the same. Not for me. You can't teach an old dog new tricks.

In some ways, I've led a sheltered life. I've never much dialogued with a scientist about religion. That's why I've become a little suspicious, assuming all science is arrayed against biblical truth. I mean, ever since Darwin, I've supposed that a scientist and a devout Christian was a contradiction in terms. Miles, for instance, is a case in point.

Of course, I knew that was not always the case. Still, I anticipated that Shino would stumble over something like Jesus's miracles. Must not the supernatural represent an insurmountable obstacle for a scientist like him? I was surprised to hear him say, "If Jesus was what he was, I don't see why he couldn't perform them." I slipped past the Genesis six-day Creation story, briefly noting that many theologians do not understand it as a scientific account of the world's origin.

Instead, I said "The Bible is as up-to-date about human nature as this morning's newspaper," when I turned to the Genesis story of the Fall. "Look what Adam did when God caught him, so to speak, with his pants down—physically naked, spiritually nude. He blamed his wife, like I blame Gertraud when I can't find our car keys I've misplaced. And then Adam blamed God with 'the woman *you* put here with me.' See, God is always to blame. And then ancient Eve finds a scapegoat, as though to say, 'The devil made me do it.' Same today, Shino. All this buck-passing, anything to escape God fingering me when he closes all avenues of escape with his 'no excuses.'" Shino had to agree, or at least he nodded so.

I got over my suspicions about science and during the following weeks discussed the major facets of the Christian faith. We took up, in succession, one topic each week. Some of the discussion I can remember.

We talked about *sin*. I avoided using the word because it has lost much of its cutting edge nowadays. "It's such a shopworn term," I told Shino, "that many regard it as a slight slip off the straight and narrow, which simply amuses God, you know, like a good-natured grandfather laughs off pranks of his well-meaning grandchildren." For better or for worse, I substituted instead, saying, "Something has gone haywire in our world, in our lives, causing this messy strife and discord we're in, don't you think, Shino?" It was easy for Shino to agree with that.

"It's something that aggravates God, to say the least. Moreover, all the 'don'ts' of the Bible can't prevent the strife very well either. Take the Ten Commandments, for instance. A little girl once said, 'They don't tell you what you ought to do.' She meant they're mostly negative: don't murder, don't commit adultery, don't steal, don't lie, don't covet. Why so negative?" I asked. And then I answered, "Because they know something about me, the kind of person I am. They head me off, like stop signs, from going where I'm inclined to go, if I could, or if I wouldn't get caught. These 'negatives' prevent me from wandering around in my neighbor's territory, where I shouldn't go, by erecting No Trespassing signs. See what I mean?"

Shino stared silently off into space, out the window. Was he agreeing with me on that point, or disagreeing? It was always hard to tell, what with that passive look on his face.

"Notice, Shino, these signs don't always work," I went on, disregarding his stare for the moment. "That's why the little girl also added, 'And they just put ideas in my head.'" Shino looked perplexed. "Put ideas in her head?" "Haven't you ever done something amiss just because, *because*, you were told *not* to? I have. I'm a little rebel. No one's going to tell me, 'Don't!'" Harking back to the Genesis story, I confessed, "I've swiped many a forbidden fruit from God's sacred tree despite his warning, 'Hands off.'" Then I said, "We are rebels with weapons in our hands," remembering a quote I had heard from someone somewhere.

We talked about *Jesus*. I introduced Jesus's work for us with the word "atonement." I broke the word into pieces with, "Jesus has made us at one with God." "How?" asked Shino. I simplified the familiar words for Jesus like "redeemer" and "reconciler" with what a boy once said, "Jesus took the rap for us." "The rap?" Shino asked, puzzled. "It's an expression, Shino, one of those idioms we use. It means to take the blame, shoulder the responsibility."

One of my favorite writers described herself with—and I quoted it to Shino—"My mind is a bad neighborhood, which I hate to enter alone."

"But we don't need to go there alone—that bad neighborhood of the mind where our conscience nags us because of bad thoughts, bad words, bad deeds. Above all, we don't need to listen to that voice that says, 'God will get you.' God already 'got you' as his child when he sent Jesus to take the rap for our bad neighborhood."

I probably did too much talking during our "classes." But Shino mainly sat there taking it all in, asking few questions, while I was wondering what was going on inside him.

We talked about *grace*. "What do you think, Shino, is it easier to forgive or to accept forgiveness?" "I know it's hard to forgive," he said. "Think about a husband who, let's say, has cheated on his wife," I said. "She forgives him. She really does. She's wonderful about it. But he can't quite believe her. So he works at it to win her forgiveness. I've seen it happen before with a couple I knew. He takes her out to dinner, buys her gifts, runs all the errands, and so forth. At least for a while."

Shino wondered what the point was. "The point is you don't have to *do* something ahead of time to receive Jesus, like go to church, say prayers, give money to the poor. That would be putting the cart before the horse. You don't pay someone for a gift, do you?" "Then it wouldn't be gift, I guess," Shino answered. "That's what grace is. It means Jesus is a gift. He's free. No strings attached. It's not like, I bet, when you persuaded your wife to marry you. Perhaps you took her out to a ball game. By the way, does she like baseball?" Shino shook his head. "No? Then, forget that. Anyway, you coaxed her, you courted her to say yes. It's different with God. His Jesus is 'on the house' as we say. It's another idiom, Shino. It means he's free. That's grace."

"I'll have to tell my wife," Shino joked, "that I did not need to do anything for her to marry me."

"No, no, Shino. That was different. Don't say that. You'll ruin everything. I'm just talking about Jesus. You don't need to woo him as we say. He's free. Get it?"

"I got it, I think," Shino said.

We talked about *faith*. The word has been so distorted in popular usage, I thought it best to describe it in negative terms.

"Faith is not subscribing to a series of various beliefs to which you must consent. We don't sign our names on a document that lists a church's teachings and call that faith. We may question some of its teachings and practices on the periphery of Christian thought, but that doesn't mean we've lost faith.

"Faith does not merely acknowledge that Jesus lived and died. Hardly anyone denies that. Not even Miles. Faith is trust that when Christ died, he did as the 'rap taker' for us. Not everyone believes that. Some make faith so complicated. It simply accepts that we have been accepted.

"Faith is not created in a vacuum. No college student of mine ever woke up some morning declaring, out of the blue, 'I'm in love.' Not unless someone he met beforehand captivated him with her beauty and charm and personality. That means faith is not man-made. It is God-made when Jesus sweeps us off our feet with his forgiving love.

"Faith is not dormant, out of work, languishingly around on welfare. It does not hang out a sign Out for Lunch or Not in Operation like you see on a storefront window or at a broken ATM. It is on the job, manufacturing articles of love to deliver free of charge to others. It is vertical because it turns upward to receive, like a child, God's grace. It is horizontal because it then turns sideways to meet the needs of a neighbor.

"Faith is never a once-and-for-all finished product like a Mercedes rolling off the assembly line. It is under attack by doubt and skepticism. That's why it needs the nourishment of God's grace. You may recall, Shino, a man in the Gospel of Mark who pleaded with Christ, 'I believe; help my unbelief.'" He remembered that from his Bible class with the Baptists.

We talked about the *sacraments*. "Here the church stands divided," I apologized to Shino. I briefly pointed out the differences that there are some Christians who baptize infants and some who do not, that there are some who confess that Christ is present in the bread and wine and some who hold a symbolic presence of Christ in those elements.

"I like to think of them as physical ways by which God brings his grace to us. God is creative. He uses all our senses to receive him. He uses our ears to hear his word of grace, our eyes to read about it. Here in the sacraments, he uses our sense of touch. They are actions. We receive his grace that he promises in the water, bread, and wine without God speaking a word. It's like when, I imagine, you hugged your sons when you left for America even if you, maybe, didn't say a word when you did. Still they felt your love, didn't they? Or when you kissed your wife good-bye at the airport. Not one of those mushy kisses, I mean, you see on television. Perhaps a final emotional one after you had already said your good-byes."

"Don't I must believe God loves me when he hugs me? You always say it takes faith." "Well, yes, of course. No, wait. Let me explain. It's yes and no. 'No' the grace of God is in that hug whether or not you believe that. Like power surging through an electric hot wire. You'll feel that power when you touch the wire. Don't try that, of course, you'll get singed. The 'yes' part is when you accept the grace offered that's already there whether or not you believed its presence."

Of course, there was much more that I said about the sacraments. But I wanted Shino to understand this one part. It seemed he did.

We talked about the *end-time*, when God brings the curtain down on human history. "What will that be like?" Shino asked. I had to admit that the New Testament provides us with few details about the afterlife. I quoted Martin Luther from my class notes under the heading Eschatology: "We know no more about eternal life than children in the womb of the mother know about the world they are about to enter."

"However," I added, "I think there are some things we can assume. It will be life with Christ when we shall see him face-to-face. It will be a life of love because love like God's love lasts forever. It will be a corporate life, life with other like-minded people because love can't exist by itself. It needs others to love. That much I think we can assume, and maybe much more."

Although I was probably "dumbing down" these teachings for Shino's sake and keeping them as simple as possible, this business about the end-time seemed to be heady stuff for him. I thought it best to let him think about it. I took a break, left the room, went down the hallway for a drink, lingered around the water fountain, came back.

Shino appeared ready for the "much more" I had left out. I said, "There will be a new creation with resurrected bodies, our feet on something material, not like wispy beings floating through the air strumming on harps. Who wants that? Boring!"

Well, our crash course was over. I had done the best I could, I thought, under the circumstances. So had Shino. He was a focused listener, with some questions and comments here and there to keep *me* focused on the topic at hand. There was no "decision" he announced about Christianity, as though we were conducting a Billy Graham revival. Nor did I ask for one. The jury was still out on that.

Before we finished the hour, I asked Shino, "You're so interested in these matters. Why aren't the others, Miles and Chen? Why aren't they as interested as you are?" "They just don't want to think about it," he said.

As we were leaving the room and heading for the church exit, I asked, "By the way, what are you going to do about your car, your Ford Taurus? You'll have to sell it before you leave, won't you?"

"You interested?" Shino asked hopefully. "I think we can get along with one car although Gertraud says she'll feel isolated with only our Passat. I don't see why, but anyway, you know women. Sure, I'd be interested."

"We'll get together again before I leave, won't we?"

"Of course. More than once. We'll have plenty of time to close the deal."

Surprise! In Church with Chen

No sooner had Shino detailed why Chen and Miles did not match his interest in matters religious with "they just don't like to think about it" when within the week, Chen proved him wrong. Of course, he was correct about Miles. Well, that has to be modified some. True enough, Miles thought about God questions. Not for long, though. Or with any serious intent. Science seemed to be his god. He never went so far as to say with Karl Marx, "Religion is the opium of the people," but that is probably close to how he felt.

Chen was different. Her mind was not locked shut. There were hints here and there that she left the door open a crack. Why had she asked me to pray to God on her behalf for this or that, why dropped in on some early sessions we had about the Bible, why attended one of the crash course sessions with Shino, why noticed a crucifix on a necklace in a jewelry store window we passed one day on an outing in Grand Haven? She just had to needle me then with, "Did you buy something like that for Gertraud when you got engaged?" I wiggled out of that one with, "She doesn't like jewelry," which was more or less true.

Then there was the time she informed me she had read the first three Gospels. She noticed the similarities in wording and said, "They must have copied each other." That was a shrewd observation that indicated she had done some serious study of the Gospels. I tried to explain why the similarities and the interrelationship between the Gospels.

Anyway, Chen was different, and Shino had seemingly mistaken about her religious frame of mind. As though she had overheard Shino's remark and wanted to set the record straight, Chen e-mailed me concerning a Chinese worship service on a Sunday afternoon—a Lutheran church, she wrote. Some festivities were planned after the service. She wanted me to join her.

What was I reading? A *Lutheran Chinese* service? There weren't any Chinese Lutherans meeting anywhere at all in Grand Rapids as far as I could tell. I phoned Kathy and asked her if she knew what Chen might have meant. Befuddled as I was, Kathy thought Chen probably meant a Pentecostal church somewhere. I phoned two of my fellow clergy, and they came up with much the same response. I searched the telephone book for an address and consulted the directories of other Lutheran Church bodies. Were any of them sponsoring a Chinese mission station? I drew a blank after each inquiry.

I e-mailed Chen, thanked her for the invitation, and wrote that I regretfully had a conflict that afternoon that I couldn't get out of. "Please invite me the next time you attend the service."

It so happened that there was a little Protestant church down a street off Burton Avenue, around a corner at the end of the lane. A Baptist church—not a Lutheran one—had rented the building as far as I could see from another Protestant church body for their Chinese services Sunday afternoons. (Chen didn't differentiate between Lutheran, Baptist, and other Protestants at the time.) Several weeks later, I had agreed to meet her for their worship.

I had planned to arrive a good ten minutes early. But why did the traffic light insist in turning red each and every time I approached an intersection? Also, heavy traffic further delayed me, as it did Chen. We both arrived in the nick of time minutes before the service began. We hurriedly took our seats next to each other. One of the ushers provided me with a headset where I heard the service in Chinese simultaneously translated in English. At one point in the service, we sang "Amazing Grace," I in English, she in Chinese. I noted how fervently she sang. To say the least, I was surprised, pleasantly surprised.

I know, I know, singing a hymn, even "Amazing Grace," didn't of itself mean that Chen had become a Christian or that she was ready for baptism. I may practice meditation, but that doesn't make me a Buddhist, much less a Buddhist monk. There are those who sing "Silent Night" at Christmas or the "Hallelujah" chorus at Easter simply because they are swept up in the mood of the moment. Still, sitting with Chen at worship and listening to her sing, I couldn't help but think, *Is this the same young lady who warned me at one of our first ESL classes, "Just don't try to make a Christian out of me"?*

The preacher's sermon wasn't very conversational in tone or folksy or filled with catchy witticisms and humorous asides. That was fine with me. Even his stern demeanor and a full-throated, straight-from-the-shoulder ringing delivery (so different from most preaching today—a little old-fashioned, I would say) was fine with me. That's saying something because we preachers, if we are frank to admit it, are the hardest to preach to. We often listen not as worshipers taking the message to heart, but as professionals to criticize. I am one of them.

I say, all that was nevertheless fine with me because his message was a Bible-based, Christ-centered study of how a man came to faith in three stages. A timely message, I hoped, for Chen. How would she react?

The preacher took the story of the man born blind in John chapter 9. Jesus repairs his sight, gives him back his vision, and then the others ask him to identify his healer. Answer: "The man they call Jesus." Simple enough. Chen would have said the same. Then the man's hostile interrogators, those and others who are "blind in the heart," as the preacher described them, demand the man to describe Jesus more specifically. Answer: "He is a prophet." Perhaps Chen would have conceded that. Finally, toward the end of the chapter, he meets up with Jesus, and in response to Jesus's question, "Do you believe in the Son of Man?" he confesses, "Lord, I believe."

So. What was I to make of this? Would Chen, too, confess the same? What was she thinking, if anything, as the pastor unfolded the whole process of coming to faith?

When we filed out of our seats, Chen introduced me to the pastor, the pastor's wife, some of the other members, and a friend or two, some from Van Andel, some from her other contacts. Chen had evidently developed a web of Christian relationships in that church and some from elsewhere. From all the hubbub of mingling with the group and conversing with them all, I was unable to interrupt with the question, "What do you think, Chen, was Jesus 'the man,' 'a prophet,' 'the Lord'?"

Before I could corner her with my question, Chen led me away to introduce me to an elderly couple from the downtown Methodist Church, whom she had also invited. They had sat behind us. When asked to introduce themselves, they indicated their delight in joining with these Chinese Christians in worship. "Why didn't you introduce yourself?" Chen asked me, disappointed. I should have. I guess the whole experience had left me tongue-tied. Or maybe I'm too shy.

"How did you come to know this couple?" I asked Chen. "I met them at their church when I heard of an invitation to an evening dinner for international students." "You aren't an international student," I said. "I know, but I went anyway. I have even visited with them in their home."

Clearly, there was a good deal about Chen's church ties I was unaware of over the past months. Clearly, Shino wasn't either. You couldn't quite include her with Miles—could you—and say about her religious interest what Shino said, "They just don't like to think about it."

Shino Decides and Departs

A week or so after the church service with Chen, Shino and I met to finalize the car deal we had agreed on. Gertraud was out of the town at the time—in fact, out of the country, back to Germany to visit her siblings.

On a Saturday afternoon, Shino drove his Ford to our condo. He had completed all the paperwork down to the very last detail. All that I had to do was to sign my name, which I managed to do. He explained how all the images on the dashboard worked, which keys fitted which locks, opened the trunk to reveal the extra motor oil and windshield-washer containers he left for me. He had the Taurus checked out at Tuffy's to ensure he wasn't hornswoggling me with a defective auto. Shino is so perfectly precise and trustworthy in matters like these; I'd go so far even to trust my very life to him—almost.

I presented him with a check for $1,000. "I'm pretty sure it won't bounce," I said laughingly. "I'm sure it won't," he said, thanking me.

We chatted for a while. Then I suggested, "It's so nice out. Let's take a walk in the park alongside the Thornapple River. What do you say? Or are you in a hurry to get back to Van Andel?" "No, no," he answered. "Good idea. We should go for walk."

We hopped into his Ford (or rather mine now) and drove to the park, a mere five minutes away. We ambled on the walk along the Thornapple. He had never been there before. When we passed by the dam in the river, I said, "I suppose it's there to control the flow of the river. Or maybe to generate electricity. I'll have to ask about that some time."

I did most of the talking because Shino's mind was somewhere else. I tried to fill in the gaps between his brief two- to three-word responses of, "That's nice," "I see," "How interesting." I couldn't sustain an extended dialogue about baseball or cancer research or the Japanese economy because Shino was in a pensive mood. I didn't expect he'd talk my ear off because Shino isn't the yakety type. Still, he was unusually quiet. His mind was working in a different gear than mine.

Suddenly, as though he had been building up for this, he said, "Paul, I have decided to become a Christian."

"What? What did you say?" He repeated, "I have decided to become a Christian." "Really? That's wonderful. Congratulations. I've frankly been wondering."

"Now what do I do?" he asked. "What do you do? You don't do anything. You've decided, and that's it. Simple as that. You don't need to write your name in some book if that's what you mean." He assumed, I guess, he had to register his name somewhere, perhaps at our church or its national headquarters.

Then he reminded me, "Don't I need to be baptized?" "Well, of course," I agreed. "Would you and Gertraud be there?" "We'd be honored to attend." He was obviously pleased. "This calls for a celebration," I said. "How about I take you to Rose's for dinner? OK?"

The waitress presented us with a menu. Shino examined the offerings and delayed and delayed in making a choice. I knew what he was doing. "Order anything you like," I insisted, "and quit looking at the prices." Of course, he was looking at the prices. That's what he always does. It would kill him to take advantage of someone's pocketbook and indulge himself with a pricey meal even if Warren Buffet were his host.

Finally, I took the bull by the horns and ordered my favorite simple hamburger plate with french fries. "I'll take the same," Shino ordered. That's just what I expected. I could have read his mind: *Nothing more expensive than Paul's.* "Please, Shino, take something better. I'm just addicted to this hamburger plate." "No, this is just fine." "I'm going to have some thing to drink. How about you, Shino? Some scotch?" "I'll just take water." Just water! Why would I have expected he'd have anything other than that—just water!

I drove Shino back downtown and dropped him off at his apartment. "Aren't you going to feel a little naked? I mean, with no car to get around?"

I asked. "It doesn't matter," he said, "I can do without it." It didn't matter because he was leaving for Japan in a few weeks. "I'll see you Thursday," I reminded him. It would be my final ESL class with him.

That Thursday, I was seated on the steps inside the church entrance waiting for my three to arrive.

Shino was the first to appear. He hurried through the entrance and rushed toward me. I could see the turmoil boiling up in my usually-composed Pool.

"Look at you, Shino. What's wrong?"

"I'm so sorry, so embarrassed."

"Why? What did you do?"

"My wife won't let me get baptized," he blurted out. "I'm so embarrassed."

"She won't? I don't understand. Why not?" I assumed she had profound theological disagreements with Christianity, and I might need to help Shino with some responses.

It was much more serious than that. At least for her.

"She says that if I get baptized, I could not be buried with her and their family in Buddhist cemetery." Their entire family—she meant parents, grandparents, grandchildren, the complete family tree—needed to be together in a Buddhist cemetery uncorrupted by a Christian presence. An absolute must! This I had forgotten about Japanese families: they are joined at the hip, wrapped together around each other like bark on a tree. And what God has joined together, let not burial plots rend asunder.

So I had to consider: should Shino get baptized and have a divorce on his hands when he returned to her? I didn't want that for them. Shino didn't either. Getting baptized on the sly, in secret without her knowledge, was out of the question. At least as far as I was concerned.

"Well then. Don't push it. Postpone baptism for now. When you return to Japan, don't argue. Just let your Christianity rub off on her. Maybe she'll come to feel the way you do."

Years ago, I had a beautiful young lady in class, a devout Christian, whose parents' marriage had ended in an acrimonious divorce. It left her devastated. Upon graduation, she moved to Japan for church work, fell in love with a Japanese, came back to be married in our college chapel at which I officiated. They married even though he was a Shinto and she still a committed Christian. He had agreed with her insistence that their children would be baptized. "Just don't shove Christianity down my throat," she told me he demanded. "What attracted you to him?" I asked her. It was certainly his charm, good looks, bright mind. But there was something more—and something better. It was his happy, harmonious family life she had witnessed—children, parents, grandparents tied together as one, like many peas in a single pod.

That was the trump card for her.

There's a lesson in that.

Shino was scheduled to fly back to Japan during the very weeks we would be on vacation at Glen Lake early in July. We decided to meet one more time after our final ESL class together to sort of wrap things up. We met in the same small room at church where we had met for our crash course. We both tried not to be so melancholy about it even though this would be our final farewell. I knew this would be the first step in the breakup of my adventure with my three friends.

There really wasn't much to talk about except to chat a little about his newfound faith. "I'm worried about you, Shino," I told him. "You'll have no support system when you get back. I don't know of any church near where you live in Japan." He just gave me a reassuring smile that said, "Not to worry." There wasn't much more to discuss, so I asked, "Do you want to pray?" He folded his hand and bowed his head while I prayed for his safe return and for God to keep him in his grace.

I'm not the hugging type. I'm not sure Shino is either. But when I drove him back to his apartment that night, we hugged each other in the parking lot for a few seconds without exchanging a word. I stood watching Shino disappear into his apartment.

They Are Dangerous!

I met Chen's husband, Bin, and their three-year-old son Kerry when they came over from Shanghai to the States. It was during the first January of our ESL classes. They somehow squeezed for the entire month into Chen's small downtown apartment—the one where Chen invited Mike and me to discuss purgatory. That topic never came up as you might remember.

Bin was tall like Chen—and handsome! He was no exception to the rule that all Chinese are required by the government to grow jet-black hair. "How come it's always black hair?" I once asked Miles. "It's genetic," he said.

We invited all three to our place for an evening, and it was good to see the family reunited for now. "How could they stand this lengthy separation?" Gertraud and I often asked ourselves. And how could Chen endure being apart from her young son? It would be one thing if Kerry were an ill-mannered, rambunctious brat, jumping up and down on our couch, ransacking the refrigerator, running through our condo, emerging from our bedroom with, "Look what I've found, Mommy." Instead, as we say, he was the sort of child you'd want as your own. Bin and Chen knew a thing or two about how to rear their son.

This January visit was exploratory in nature, we realized, when Chen expressed the hope that Bin would find employment in Grand Rapids, and they would make America their permanent home—at least for the foreseeable future. I'm only guessing now, but wouldn't you think Chen's decision to come to America precipitated some disagreement about her move? After all, Chen had dropped some hints to me about a difference of opinion between the two about the matter.

And what to do about Kerry? Does Chen just casually say good-bye to her son as though she were devoid of all maternal instincts? I doubt that, knowing Chen as I do. I think it's different with the Chinese. I'm convinced they handle these family separations without getting into a knock-down, drag-out argument. Whatever the case may have been, this was their private business. For once, I resolved not to stick my nose into it.

Anyway, Bin was here for a visit with Kerry. To repeat: the plan was for Bin to find employment here in Grand Rapids. He arrived with colorful brochures displaying his work as a building engineer.

However, two major problems stood in the way. First, despite the efforts on the part of some professional friends, the possibility of a position for Bin became remote, to say the least. (The proverbial finding a needle in a haystack applies here.) Second, Bin's grasp of the English language was about as proficient as mine was of Chinese, which is to say nonexistent. Bin left for China with Kerry the end of January. Over the succeeding months, the attempt to find employment for Bin was a flop.

Time passed. The family problem was apparently resolved. And Chen returned from a visit in China with Kerry in hand the months before Shino left. "Now," Chen jubilantly reported, "I finally feel like a mother."

They lived together in Chen's small apartment, and Kerry attended a downtown preschool, with Chen shuttling back and forth from work to pick him up. It was not an ideal arrangement. I don't know how she managed it.

Kerry was soon ready for the first grade, and Chen wanted the best schools for him. The best schools were in our area. Chen resolved to enroll Kerry in one of them and to relocate in a more spacious apartment—not far from us as it happened—where Kerry would have easy access to schools. This would mean up-and-at-it early mornings for both of them involving Kerry in a school bus transfer and Chen a long drive to Van Andel.

How to find an apartment? What school to enroll Kerry?

Chen seemingly didn't determine to resolve these complications beforehand. I would have. Obsessive as I am, I would have considered every eventuality and prearranged every detail before moving my child thousands of miles to what—it would mean for Kerry certainly—a foreign country. But I'm not a mother. And I'm not Chen. This self-sufficient Swan simply dove into these murky waters confident she would emerge on solid ground. The controlling motive was, more than anything else, that Chen wanted to be a mother, and she wanted the best for her son.

Of course, Chen had help. Gertraud's friend, Julie, a longtime resident here, knew where apartments were located in our general area. And Kathy, ever-helpful Kathy, spent hours driving Chen around Cascade Township searching for schools and apartments. This effort is not to be underrated. Chen needed a suitable apartment not too distant from a school prepared to help Kerry, who spoke little English. A little complicated in finding the right fit for the two of them.

After one of Kathy's safaris with Chen throughout Cascade Township, hunting down schools and apartments, Kathy returned to church. She had been gone for three hours and was met by someone at the church who asked, "Where have you been?" It was an innocent inquiry, not a demand to account for her time away.

"I was driving around with Chen, looking for an apartment for her."

"Chen? Who is Chen?"

"One of our ESL students. A Chinese. She's a scientist next door at Van Andel."

"A Chinese? How long were you with her in the car?"

"For three hours or thereabouts, I guess."

"Three hours? Really, *three hours?*"

"Why, yes. Three hours more or less. Why do you ask?"

"Were you *alone* with her?"

"Yeah, sure. All alone. Her son was in school. Is there a problem?"

"You mean *all alone* with her, in a car, for three whole hours?"

The man was kidding, Kathy assumed, his sort of dry humor at work. So Kathy started laughing.

"No, don't laugh," he said. "I'm not kidding."

"What do you mean? You were kidding, weren't you?"

"No, I'm serious. All alone with her! For three hours! I don't trust those people. They're communistic."

"What? What did you say?"

"I just do not trust those people. They're *dangerous!*"

Can you imagine that? *I don't trust those people. They're dangerous.*

Chen, it must be assumed, had plotted to abduct Kathy and hold her for ransom, or was a member of the Chinese mafia fomenting crime and corruption in our society, or researched how to implant cancer cells in unsuspecting United States citizens.

Moreover, Kathy endangered her own life by accompanying someone, I suppose, quite possibly a devotee and admirer of Mao Tse-Tung. You are forced to imagine that such sinister suspicions occupy the thoughts of some fearful folks whose minds become unhinged at the sight of a Chinese.

An isolated case? Let's go on.

Soon after that incident one Thursday evening, I was quietly minding my own business in the church's hallway awaiting the arrival of my ESL class. A young lady, perhaps in her early thirties, one whom I had never met before, a stranger, happened by. She wondered what I was up to.

"Teaching English to Van Andel scientists."

"Any foreign students?"

"Why, yes, of course. That's why they're learning English."

"I suppose they're Asians, some of them."

"They *all* are. Three of them. One Japanese, two Chinese."

How shocking! You could almost hear alarm bells reverberating in her head. The mention of a Japanese, she took right in stride. But Chinese? And *two* of them?

Then, as though she were a CIA agent, she said this solemn word to the wise, "You know, don't you, they're *dangerous!*"

Since she seemed to be sound in mind otherwise, with no apparent mental defects, well dressed, perhaps a college graduate, I tried to take the edge off her concern about my two Chinese friends with, "You must mean the Chinese government itself. You think their leaders are a threat."

"No, the Chinese in general. They're *dangerous.*" (Not again!)

Come now! Has it come to *that* with some people?

I was at first furious. Then bewildered. "What is wrong with these people? Such unenlightened close-mindedness. They need to get out more."

Self-righteously, I measured myself against them. *I* am not that way. *I* am not warped with prejudice. *I* am not xenophobic. Of course, I'm not because I've had the opportunity—and I must add the privilege—of visiting with Chen in our place and hers, cordially exchanging views with her, partying with her, receiving gifts from her, attending social functions with her, and yes, drinking scotch with her. The same goes for Miles—except for the scotch.

In other words, familiarity did not breed contempt despite our differences.

I used to be intimidated by my daughter's mean-spirited dog, a snarling dachshund, barking, snapping, growling at me. That is, until I lowered myself to his level, gave him his favorite morsel in my open hand, petted his head, rubbed his tummy, threw his rubber ball for him to chase, played with him.

And you know what? We became friends.

Are Miles and Chen Next?

Shino left for Japan while Gertraud and I were on vacation at Glen Lake the first two weeks of July. I told Shino I'd wave to him by the lakeside as he flew over us. I wasn't sure which exact day he was leaving during those two weeks. So I waved each day. I'm not sure he saw me.

I call it a vacation, which is something of a misnomer because we're retired. Who needs a vacation while retired? I should rather call it something like a pause, a sort of recess from class, my ESL class. It was a time to reflect about my Asian threesome: what would our class be like without Shino? One wheel had fallen off the tricycle I was riding. Now that Chen was further occupied with Kerry under her wing—and a mother's job is never done, you know—would hers be the next wheel to detach itself?

As for Miles—well, you never know about Miles. What was this restless Bumblebee planning for his future career? Several presentations at major events were on his résumé. He was in a position to flirt for a more prestigious position elsewhere in the USA. Sadly, one member had already left "this odd but perfect mixture of personalities." What about these other two?

On that July, there were several reasons why I suspected Miles would be the first of the remaining two to "defect." On one hand, he spoke English fairly well. Despite occasional mispronunciations, several grammatical gaffes, and a few semantic foul-ups, I doubted if it was worth his time to perfect his English in class. In his line of work, was it really necessary? He wanted to research, not teach. Nor would he be making formal speeches or writing lengthy essays that required polished English.

Additionally, how he grasped the point of stories—O. Henry's "The Last Leaf" for instance—was impressive! Would he catch on to the point made at the conclusion of Henry's marvelous short story? He did, to my surprise, when after reading it out loud, he looked up at me and said, "Wow! Marvelous!" Did Miles really need to remain in class to improve his English? Probably not. But I wasn't going to tell him. I didn't want him to leave too. A little selfish, you'd say.

Another reason I suspected Miles would drop out was the chat we had before a class began. He arrived earlier than normally, as I did, and we were alone. This time there was none of his bouncing into the classroom, opening windows, arranging chairs, taking charge as usual, with that dimpled smile from ear to ear. This time his mood was thoughtful, subdued. Usually, I'd first tease him about something or other, or we would estimate how old Chen might be. Not now though. I could tell this was not the time for that.

He was in a serious mood because he was "weighing an offer" as he put it. China needed the head administrator of a hospital or some other similar institution—I wasn't clear which he meant—and the offer was his. He planned to leave for China, investigate the possibility for a week, and then return with his decision.

It was a dilemma for him because as he said, "If I accept offer from my homeland, I can do much good for my own people. But if I stay here and do cancer research, I can do more for people in world." He didn't ask for my advice, and I didn't give him any. I don't think you do that with Miles anyway. Of course, I'd rather have him stay here even if it meant he'd drop out of class. The latter would be the lesser of two evils for me.

This "weighing an offer" did not involve an income increase or career advancement. At least, he never even hinted that those factors entered into his thinking. What concerned him was where he could best use his abilities. That convinced me he was a genuine humanitarian. He had a heart for people. He has shown that side of his before. I wondered where he got that. Maybe from his parents. I know it wasn't from religion. He has shown that side of his before too. The very fact that he should even weigh the particular concern for his fellow Chinese over against the universal regard for all humanity made him something special in my eyes. You have to admire that in Miles.

What about Lin? She had just completed her degree in accounting at Western Michigan University. I asked, "What could she do with that degree in China? What if accounting practices she learned here wouldn't conform to practices in China? What would there be for her to do over there, then?" Maybe Miles suspected I was erecting obstacles to convince him to turn down the offer, for that is what, to be honest, I was doing. Miles wrote off that potential problem for Lin and showed the kind of stuff she was made of when he responded curtly, "She's flexible."

I felt more secure about Chen. That is, there wasn't any sign that she was planning to return to China. In fact, the evidence pointed in the other direction.

One evening, at our place, we visited alone with Kerry along. Gertraud was busy with Kerry in the living room, and Chen sat across from me in the family room. Without any fanfare but with obvious pride, she said, "Paul, I have something to tell you. I am promoted. I am now official member of faculty at Van Andel."

"You don't say! My goodness. Good for you. You must be famous." "No, oh no. Just on faculty." "Promoted in such a short time you're here?" I admired. "You're on the rise. Someday you'll be famous. I'll be able to tell people, 'I know her!'" She smiled away the compliment as though to say, "Not famous ever. Won't happen."

What bothered her was that she now had assistants, all American graduate students, and she worried about communicating with them. "Would you help me?" she asked. "I don't know their culture—how they talk." What she meant was their American slang, the jargon they had picked up in college. Moreover, she said, "They may not understand my English. I get things wrong. My English is not always right."

"We have an ophthalmologist, a Chinese, whose accent is so strong," I told Chen, "that we can half understand him. He hasn't bothered much to try to improve over the years. Right from the start, his assistants told us they would explain what he meant. If I were you, I wouldn't worry about it. Your English is plenty good enough. If you don't catch on to their lingo, tell them to say again—only in clearer English. After all, you're in charge, not they."

Chen is such a gifted scientist, I'm sure she'll make something of herself. Perhaps will really become famous despite her denial. All the signs suggested she'll do it here in America, maybe even right here in Grand Rapids.

Her promotion reassured me. Our truncated class will hang together in the hope that Miles will be back for good. It won't be exactly the same without Shino. We'll meet as though Shino was in absentia. Maybe we can find another Asian that would somewhat resemble him, although there's only one Shino.

Homophobia

Miles returned from his jaunt to China to announce that he had declined the offer. He revealed no details, nor was there any sign that he agonized over his decision. But it seemed to me the offer itself meant he was a wanted commodity in China and that this was not the last time they'd be after him.

I was concerned that this was a sign of things to come.

When the Asian scientists decide to join our ESL program, Kathy interviews them to determine their level of English proficiency and then assigns them to the appropriate class. Miles ignored that formality and took it upon himself, his first class back, to take matters in his own hands. Chen was gone that week, away on some project out of town. Not surprisingly, Miles, in his wisdom, decided to fill out our class and, bypassing Kathy's interview, invited, or rather assigned, two more to the class: Hideaki and Xin.

Hideaki, whose name I shortened to Hide, was studying for his PhD at the same medical college where Shino was the professor. "He's the best teacher of all," Hide informed me, which did not surprise me. Hide was thirty-seven years old although, like so many of the Japanese, looked ten years younger. Unlike Shino and others, Hide was here with his wife, Kayomi, and their three children. Hide's grasp of English didn't qualify him for our book 7 lessons—as even Chen later pointed out to me—but he made up for that deficiency by his fondness for scotch, which he freely imbibed at a party with these newcomers. Perhaps that is why he gifted me with an ornate scotch glass before he left for Japan several months later.

They tried to get me to pronounce Xin's name correctly, with something that sounded like "Sheen." That didn't sound to me like the equivalent of "Xin" in English and unnecessarily too long. So I called him Sin. Unfortunately, that provided Miles with one of his religious *digs*. "Paul likes that word," he laughed.

Sin was ten years younger that Hide, an MD studying for his PhD at Nanking Medical University. Unlike Hide, he spoke fluent English. Although he had a girlfriend back home as Chen informed me (how does she know all these things?), we suggested good-naturedly that he might consider marrying an American. He had the driest sense of humor of all and quick as a whip when he sparred with Kathy and me about what he required in an American bride.

"Does she have to have a PhD?"

"Preferably yes, but she should not be smarter than me."

"Beautiful? Good figure?"

"Yes, of course, but not taller than me," which would have been a challenge because he was somewhat short.

"How about money? Does she have to be rich?"

"Lots and lots of money."

"What if she had some abnormality, say something gross like three legs?"

"I prefer she had only two."

Along with Hide, he was due to leave Van Andel in several months. "Will they throw a party for you when you leave?" I asked. "No, of course not. I'm not that important." "Well, I will. I'll take you out to dinner," which I did the night before he left. He presented me then with a beautiful triptych containing colorful Chinese emblems.

I enveloped him in a big hug when I dropped him off at his apartment. We promised to e-mail each other when he returned to China.

Now, that's a little ahead of our story. Before Sin departed, the class attacked lesson 15, which contained Ernest Hemingway's "A Day's Wait." The three of them took turns reading the story (Hide fumbled here and there with the English) and completed the first five exercises until we came to exercise 6 entitled Homonyms. The book explained that homonyms "are words that sound alike but are different in spelling and meaning," like "lessen" and "lesson," like "aid" and "aide."

We accidently stumbled into a moral issue when I tried to explain the derivation of homonym. "The first part of the word comes from the Greek 'homo,' meaning the same, and the second part means—"

"Like homosexual," interrupted Miles.

Well then, OK, I decided since Miles brought it up, let's get into this matter and see how comfortable these Asians are about it.

"Homosexuals," I began. "They're fairly out in the open in places here in America. I've even seen groups of them in Chicago on a street corner, holding hands, even kissing each other." Then I zeroed the issue in on them. "Are there any in China or Japan?"

Hide shrugged his shoulders into an "I don't know," obviously distancing himself from the subject. Sin thought that perhaps there might be some in China, though he wasn't quite sure. The looks on their faces said, "Don't look at me. I'm not one of them." (Sounds like some homophobia at work here.) Miles, always brutally honest, said, "Of course, there are. Only they're not out in the open." I assumed he knew the facts. Later I learned from a *Time* magazine article that "homosexuality was—and still is—very much in the closet in China; Beijing had just taken it off an official list of mental disorders." Seems like Miles knew what he was talking about.

"Are they so by nature or by nurture? I mean, are they that way from birth, or did they learn it from their environment? What do you think?" I asked them.

"By nature! They're born that way. They can't help it," Miles said authoritatively, drawing from his accumulated reservoir of knowledge about everything. "That's good," he declared, "because diversity is good for society."

That settled the question without further comment from Hide or Sin. I gathered they were ill at ease about the subject. "Now let's go on with the lesson," Miles directed.

Miles handled this issue the same way he did after the Luther movie where Luther differed with church and state. If there are dissimilarities in religion, or here, with sexual outlook, that's always good for society according to the doctor. Diversity is what matters.

"Wait a minute," I said, stopping Miles's directive to continue in midair. "There's the word 'bisexual.' What about that? Are some people bisexual in your countries?"

"You mean some who like both sexes at the same time?" asked Sin, acting surprised. I surmised he knew but was feigning ignorance.

"Uh-huh," I answered. "I've heard of some, or rather one person, who was married, even had children. He wanted it both ways. Then his wife divorced him. He died later, I was told, of a heart attack. It was probably caused by AIDS. Sad story. So, yes, there are some who are bisexual. At least they try to be—in practice."

I worried that Hide, married with his three children, might think I had him in mind as a possibility. "Don't worry, Hide," I said. "I'm not thinking of you."

For once, Miles had no authoritative word to proclaim about bisexuality. "Let's finish the lesson," he repeated.

Maybe I shouldn't have gotten into this whole issue. I blame it on Miles as I usually do. But it was interesting to see how our two cultures were more or less mirror images of each other. Perhaps some homophobia with two of them. Blunt open-mindedness about homosexuality with Miles.

The ESL Breakup

My ESL life with Chen and Miles came to an abrupt end the last of August, one year after Shino left. It was the final act (a little like the "death scene" for me) in a drama filled with skits and routines I played with my Asian friends: classes, parties, movies. Also, let's not forget Chen's adventures with her Toyota, her traffic violations, and her court appearances. What began with "strangers within our gates" in the parlors of Immanuel Lutheran one Thursday evening ended this summer day with "friends," not students but friends, the closest thing to family members.

"Paul," Miles announced in class, "I won't be able to attend class anymore—not at least until after Christmas. We have big project we must finish end of year. Lots of pressure. I need more time for work."

But it would be much more than that that would end ESL for Miles.

I never thought of Miles as a family man. I always had the feeling he didn't want children. Mice and test tubes and microscopes were his children. However, Chen let the cat out of the bag when earlier that summer, she told me Lin was pregnant. Chen had become my chief informer on events outside class, who kept me up-to-date on important developments. This was one of them. She explained Lin's pregnancy by quoting Lin's demand to Miles, "I want a baby!"

The baby was due by Christmas. So what was Miles thinking—that he would have *more time then* for class with a baby in their apartment? Hardly. After our first child was born, a mother informed me, "From now on your life will change by seventy-five percent." I guess Miles didn't count on that. No, his presence in class would be over for good.

Turned out, after Christmas, it was.

Simultaneously with Miles's announcement, Chen echoed the same report. "You too busy also?" I asked Chen. "A big project as well?" "Well, yes, but not that so much. I need to be home with Kerry at night. Can't leave him alone." I could understand that. It was inevitable. Kerry was as bright as could be, but there was his homework for Chen to supervise and his English for her to help with.

I added Miles and Chen to Shino's permanently retired list. That ended ESL for the two of them. And all within five minutes.

I kept contact with Chen through e-mails after that. There was the repeated problem with tires for her Toyota and its assorted ailments she asked me about. "My car is making funny sound," she e-mailed me. The Toyota dealer said she needed a new tire, which will cost her $100. I recalled what my son, Gerhardt, once said, "You never buy new tires from the car dealer. They charge too much." I reminded her of the discount dealer where she earlier paid far less for new tires. "Tell me if I can help," I e-mailed her.

She handled the problem herself, but I would have loved to have been there at the Toyota dealer, where she went anyway, to hear her finagling over the price once again.

I e-mailed her, "Did you get your tires? How much did they sock you for them?"

She e-mailed me beginning with, "Paul, I hope everything is fine of you. I finally got my tires. They are willing to give me 15 percent off for both purchases and service. In addition, it is the promotion time that if I buy four tires, I will get $50 gas card."

Obviously, she had not lost her knack for haggling for the best deal. Or did they pull the wool over her eyes since she explained she was still waiting for the gas card through the mail?

She went on, "I think it is end of story, but they also suggest me to replace the timing belt as soon as possible. It cost another more $200. What does timing belt do? Do you have an idea?" Since I don't know the difference between a carburetor and the generator, I was of absolutely no help.

She concluded, "I am thinking if the story goes on, I will eventually replace my car." She did. End of Toyota adventures.

There were complications with Lin's pregnancy, and Stella was born prematurely in October. Her condition was nip and tuck, but the tiny girl survived after a lengthy stay in intensive care. Gertraud wrapped a lovely gift, and I delivered it to Miles at Van Andel. "It's great to be a father, isn't it?" I told his beaming face.

Throughout the next year, there were intermittent visits and exchanges of e-mails with Miles as there were with Chen. Our visits were separate occasions between the two of them, on one occasion with Chen and Kerry, on another with Miles and Lin. The plus side was that we were able to devote more time with each pair to learn a little more about their parents, siblings, their current work at Van Andel, their plans for the future, if any. However, I missed the lively interchange that took place when all three of them—or at the last, just the two of them—debated in class and partied over pizza.

On one such visit with Miles and Lin in late May, we sat around a table on our patio. They brought Stella, now grown and healthy, with no ill effects showing from her premature birth some seven or so months earlier. I thought she looked like Miles. Gertraud thought she looked like Lin. She definitely looked Chinese, with dark eyes and that jet-black hair—what else would you expect?

"Why the name Stella?" I asked Miles and Lin. "That's an American name, isn't it? Why not a Chinese name?" Miles provided us with some mystical explanation (which to this day Gertraud and I do not understand), something that had to do with stars in the China sky. We were afraid to ask Miles for further clarification. Who knows where that would have taken us—or for how long? My dictionary defines "Stella" in terms of a star and relates it in part to "an experimental international coin," which I suppose is close to what Miles had in mind.

We didn't realize it then, but that fall, Miles must have been planning for their exit from America and their return to China.

Another Farewell

Early the next year, to take a break from the cold Michigan winter, Gertraud and I planned a cruise. I e-mailed our Asian friends, naming the islands we would be visiting in the "warm, warm, warm Caribbean. Maybe you can find them on the map and enjoy the warm weather with us." I knew they would smile at my lame humor, knowing that I was just trying to make them a tiny bit envious. Then I included what I learned, probably from Chen, what Miles had planned all along, "I think I heard that Miles is moving back to China for good. He must not do that without my permission since I'll miss him *sooo* much."

Miles returned my e-mail with his own better wit, "Remember to tell the pirates that you are not going to rob them."

Then he concluded with his official announcement, "I am leaving the United States on April 30. After that, I will work in Singapore for twenty days and leave Singapore for China on May 20. I will contact you even when I am in China." So there. The curtain was coming down on my second U.S. contact with my foreign friends. Would Chen be the next?

Three days before Lin and Miles left, we had a farewell party for them, as we had for Shino. That morning, I e-mailed Shino: "Dear Shino, you are cordially invited for a pizza party tonight at 6:00 PM at our place for Lin and Miles who are leaving for China. I know this is short notice, but maybe if you can get on a missile, you will be able to make it."

I was pleased to see that time had not changed Shino's ability to see through my absurdity when he forthwith returned an e-mail and with a straight face wrote, "Dear Paul, thank you for your 'one day' notice. I asked the Ministry of Defense to prepare a missile in which I can get on, and they answered it is possible, but it takes a little time to get permission from the secretary of defense. In addition, the missile is an old-type one, and it may drop in the Pacific Ocean. So please start the party at 6:00 PM even if I cannot arrive on time."

If any carefree, happy-go-lucky American (as we are often viewed) should ever regard these Asians as humorless, boringly disciplined, no-nonsense *go-getters* (as I initially had), they should meet Miles and Shino.

When Miles and family entered our condo, Stella, now a vigorous two-year-old, began climbing on a chair and sliding off our couch. Usually, Gertraud takes a dim view of unprovoked attacks our furniture suffers at the hands of unruly children, but this was an exceptional occasion. Why not let us celebrate this child's robust bouncing about, who escaped a near-death experience at birth? "Look what she can do! Look what she can do!" trumpeted the proud father. "As though," Gertraud whispered to me, "he were the only father in the world."

There was the usual exchange of gifts. (These Asians never came empty-handed on a visit.) We gave them something to remember us by, a hardbound pictorial book on the state of Michigan, featuring our historic and memorable lakes, sand dunes, and lighthouses.

Miles presented me with two colorful calling cards. The one identified him as a Professor at a University Cancer Center in Southern China, with his home address at Guangzhou added. The other read National Cancer Center Singapore, where Miles was listed as deputy director. For the first time in memory, I saw his full name: Chao-Nan Qian, but with "Miles" in parenthesis inserted between "Nan" and "Qian." He won't let anyone, even in China and Singapore, ignore his "renowned" nickname.

"So you'll work at two separate places, Guangzhou and Singapore? Will you drive back and forth?" I asked.

"Look at map, Paul. They are too far apart. Over one thousand miles. Besides, impossible to drive to Singapore." (I should have studied geography better in school.)

"Not the train either, I suppose. What then?"

"You know, we have airplanes in China, Paul."

"Right. Of course. But won't that cost you a ton of money, you know, if you have to fly?"

"They will shuttle me back and forth. *All expenses paid!*" Miles crowed, his nose in the air.

"What? *All expenses paid?* Why? How did you manage that?"

"It's because I'm so important. They need me," he crowed, congratulating himself.

Lin tapped him on his head and rolled her eyes, always her way of deflating his "know-it-all."

After our "cheeseless" pizza, we reminisced about our past class sessions. I reminded him how, when in nontechnical laymen's terms, he had explained that cancer spreads when a tumor sends out "spies" to a fertile spot in the body to inhabit. Now he called them "sons and daughters."

I reminded him how I had asked him, "Why be a good person in the first place?" which he felt was the prime purpose in life, something important for all society. I attempted again this evening to get at the basic "why," the reason behind his "being good person." Maybe it had something to do with God after all, I faintly hoped. No, it derived from his parents' teaching in Thailand, he explained, which included no reference to religion, as I suspected. We came full circle again when he admitted, "There is some selfishness because what's good for society is good for me."

The evening was coming to a close when Miles surprised us with this: "We will all be coming back in six years."

"What? Coming back here to USA?"

"Yes, in six years."

"Why? And why in six years?"

"Stella will be ready for school then."

"Aren't there schools in China?" I joked. "Not that we wouldn't want to have you back."

"They don't make you think in Chinese schools. Just memorize what they say. Here they make you think."

"Really? I didn't realize the difference. You sure you're right?" Miles was sure.

I put that feather in the cap of our educational system.

There were hugs and "thank-yous" and "good-byes" as we stood at the door and then watched them drive off.

"Do you really think they'll be back in six years?" I asked Gertraud.

She shrugged her shoulders. "With Miles you never know what to expect."

Final Questions and Answers

Almost always, when Chen communicates with me outside our class sessions, she does it through e-mail. Rarely does she telephone. That's why I was surprised when later in the year a week or so before Christmas, she telephoned. I answered. "Paul," she asked, "could Kerry and I come over for cup of tea? We want to say good-bye. We are leaving for China day before Christmas."

That sounded ominous. Now that Shino and Miles had left, is this the final farewell party, the last I'll see of my Asian friends?

"Why, sure," I replied after checking with Gertraud. "How about Friday night? But let's have a light supper and some goodies. Maybe a little scotch too instead of tea," I added, dressing up this farewell party with something more than pizza.

After dinner, Chen and Kerry took their customary places on the couch in our family room. Gertraud and I sat across from them.

"So you're leaving for China," I said, sounding, I'm sure, a bit resentful.

"Yes, we will have Christmas party. Christmas tree, presents, everything we always have at Christmas."

"Well then, what about Kerry? He'll have to start all over again, won't he, in a Chinese school? To make another change, won't that be a problem for him, don't you think? Or not?"

"There is no problem. We'll be back end of January. I have big project at Van Andel. Kerry has permission to miss some time in school."

"So you're not leaving for good?"

"Why you say that? It's my vacation."

"Uh, I didn't know. I just thought that maybe, well, I don't know, that maybe you were leaving for good," I said, realizing that I had jumped the gun. "Here, have some more scotch."

"No thanks," she said. "I'm driving, you know."

Gertraud is much better with children than I am. Poor Kerry just sat there, ignored by me while I talked with Chen. That's why Gertraud centered our attention on him. She talked with him about school, his playmates, if he eats at McDonald's.

"How well Kerry speaks English," she told Chen. "No accent at all. You're keeping him up with his native tongue, I hope. You wouldn't want him to lose that, I think. Right?"

"We speak Chinese at home. It's better now for him to know English so he can play with friends. And for school, of course. He's in second grade."

"So how is he doing in school?" Gertraud asked.

"There is some test in math where the normal score for most is 300. But Kerry's score is 900."

"Wow! 900! Astounding! He must be a genius," Gertraud said.

"Let's try something in math, Kerry," I began. "Just for the fun of it. Let's see. How much is eight and eight?" "Sixteen." "Good. OK, how about sixteen and sixteen?" "Thirty-two." "What about thirty-two plus thirty-two?" "Sixty-four." "Excellent. Let's try just one more. This is difficult. You don't have to try this if you don't want. What is sixty-four and sixty-four?" He thought for a while. "Maybe one hundred twenty-eight, I guess?"

"Wait a minute," I said. "Let me think." I ran some mathematical gymnastics through my head. (Four and four are eight. Six and six are twelve. Together that's one hundred twenty-eight.)

"Right, Kerry, you're right. I tell you, Chen. Kerry is a genius."

"But I'm afraid others will consider him a nerd," Chen responded.

"A *nerd?* Where did you learn that word?"

"I talk to people. And listen. You always said that's how we learn English best."

"For once, you did what I told you," I joked. She just smiled. "By the way, Chen, do you realize how your English has improved? Just listen to you."

She ignored the compliment and came back to her worry.

"I don't want his playmates to think he's a nerd. All he does is read and read and read."

(In fact, that's what he was doing now, in the living room, by himself, reading a book he had brought along.)

"Also, he doesn't like sports," she added.

"I thought you told me once he played soccer this summer at the YMCA?"

"He did. But he doesn't like competition."

"I would not worry about that. Maybe I should take him to a ball game this summer. To one of the Whitecaps' ball games. I should probably sit down with him first and explain baseball. It's a little complicated for foreigners. We could leave after a few innings if he doesn't like it. You want to come along?"

She seemed to think it was a good idea.

Chen turned the conversation from Kerry and herself and focused all the attention on Gertraud and me. This was the first time any of the three had asked the personal questions of *when* and *where* and *how* we got married. Maybe it was due to the natural reserve that, I assumed, characterizes the Asian culture. (But can you imagine Miles be so reserved?) Or more likely, it was because we were one-on-one with each other, uninterrupted by the other two, a rare occasion.

At any rate, there were a thousand times, it seems, we were asked those questions. Chen was genuinely interested in the answers. Since Gertraud is a *German* who married an *American*, that generates considerable curiosity from people, as it did from Chen now.

The back and forth usually goes like this. I'll spare you our wordy answers.

"Where did you first meet?" (No, I wasn't in the army stationed in Germany, but when . . .)

STRANGERS WITHIN OUR GATES

"How did you meet?" (No, it wasn't at a party or through friends, but by . . .)

"When did you get married?" (Twice, on September 6 and again on the tenth, same month, same year.)

"Why twice?" (Don't ask. Too complicated a story.)

That "twice" question was the clue for an answer to "where were you married?" (On this side of the pond and on the other side.)

Then it was our turn. We asked her the same reporter's questions: how, when, where, why. However, Chen's marriage followed the more conventional route. Met through friends, got married, on one and the same day, same city, same country. Very *normal-like*, with no parental marital prearrangements, as you sometimes hear about in the East. Very *unlike* our own complex maneuvering taken to tie the knot. Ours was almost like Eisenhower planning the invasion of Normandy.

There was, however, this other matter about Chen's marriage. She's on one side of the Pacific now; her husband, on the other side. A permanent arrangement? "No," Chen later said. "Bin is still working on a visa to move and work here." It is nowadays, it appears, frustratingly wearisome, getting through government bureaucracies. Something like trying to understand the tax code.

The evening was winding down when Chen, with the force of a solemn pronouncement, said, "I have been going to church." It was at a Baptist church with some friends.

"You are? No kidding. I wish I had known that."

"Guess what? When Kerry ate lunch at the Y, they always began with prayer. When we sat down to eat at home, he'd say before we began, 'Let's pray.' First time we've done that." ("Out of the mouths of babes and infants.")

"Well, isn't that something! Did you know they got into religion at the Y?"

"He was also told that Jesus sacrificed himself for us."

I asked Kerry, sitting beside her, "Do you know what that means?" He shook his head. "No, not really."

The time was appropriate, I concluded, to ask her directly what I had never asked her before, "Are you a Christian?"

"I'm thinking about it."

"What would your father say, you know, if you became a Christian?"

"He always lets me decide for myself. What I want to do, like when I wanted to come to America."

"Even if you became a Christian? Wouldn't he object to that?"

"Like I say, he lets me be free to decide for myself."

"Tell me, Chen. In ESL. Did I ever try to make a Christian out of you?"

"No, not really. I never felt that."

"Be honest now. Did I ever try to argue you into it? Did I intimidate you, try to force it on you? Even indirectly?"

"No, *never*. Honestly." I felt vindicated.

"It doesn't happen that way anyway," I said. "Christianity is a love story. How God loves us . . . in Jesus. You can't force a person to love in return. Right?"

She nodded her agreement.

"If you want to talk more about this, if you want to know more about Christianity, let me know."

"One thing more," she said. "If I decide to become Christian, would *you* baptize me?"

"*Would I?* Of course. You just tell me when, and we'll arrange it"

I am still waiting. Chen is definitely a work in progress.

Epilogue

We've seen Chen off and on after that. Not as often as we'd like because she is so busy with Kerry and her research. She just recently applied for a $100,000 grant. I hope she gets it. I hope, too, she and Bin become permanently reunited again. I predict her name will make a mark on the cancer research field someday. I wouldn't be surprised if she'd be enticed by some prestigious position in the Big Apple, or maybe Boston, where I've heard she's had connections. On the other hand, she's purchased a home in Grand Rapids now—a sure sign she'll stay here.

I've sort of lost track of Miles. He's still in China, I'm sure, but Chen heard rumors that Lin moved back with Stella, living in an apartment in Grand Rapids. We can't seem to track down her address and telephone number. I have an inkling Lin's return is a sign something has gone amiss with Miles's work in China. Has he sent Lin ahead to prepare the way for his return, earlier than the six years he had planned on? Would Van Andel rehire him? Probably. But he has "ants in his pants." I imagine he will move on to somewhere else.

Shino returns to the United States about once a year for a week to discuss a research project at Van Andel. He has even driven to Notre Dame and the University of Chicago to discuss projects with researchers there. I'm proud to know this distinguished scholar. He sets aside one evening of each of those weeks for a visit with us. He's still a Christian, he tells me, though not yet baptized. Of course, he always arrives with presents for us.

I hope that before I go "to the other side"—as my daughter puts it—we'll coordinate our schedules and just for the sake of it have one more ESL session. I think it's about lesson 18 where we left off. Or go to a movie, with pizza afterward. What fun that would be! But I know that will never happen! It's like the three little tea candles I'd light every evening after class on the coffee table between my chair and the couch where they'd sit. I've learned to light the candles, all three of them, with just one match. Then while watching television, I'd glance over at them and watch them flicker out. Not all of them at once but first one, then another, and then the last stubborn one, which often lingers on and on. I hate it, but before I go to bed, I simply need to blow it out.

Get Published, Inc!
Thorofare, NJ 08086
19 April, 2010
BA2010109